W9-BFY-460

ALBUQUERQUE
BLAZING NEW TRAILS

TOWERING TWO MILES HIGH OVER ALBUQUERQUE at its easternmost city limits, the craggy granite slopes of the Sandia Mountains are ever changing in their visual splendor. Sandia is Spanish for watermelon, and each day just before dusk the fading sun turns the mountain's surface a bright watermelon pink. The sunsets become even more breathtaking during a thundershower or snowstorm.

Charles Ledford

AlBUQUERQUE
BLAZING NEW TRAILS

EDITOR	Rob Levin
PUBLISHER	Barry Levin
ASSOCIATE EDITORS	Julie Carroll
	Cheryl Sadler
PROJECT DIRECTOR	John Lorenzo
PHOTO EDITOR	Chuck Young
SENIOR WRITER	Rena Distasio
	Regina Roths
JACKET & BOOK DESIGN	Compōz Design Imaging
PHOTOGRAPHERS	Charles Ledford
	John F. Nugent
	Rod Reilly
	Alan Weiner
	Tim Wright
	Chuck Young

Riverbend Books wishes to thank the staff from the Greater Albuquerque Chamber of Commerce for its assistance and guidance in publishing – *Albuquerque – Blazing New Trails*. Without its support, this book would not have been possible.

RIVERBEND BOOKS
A division of BOOKHOUSE GROUP, INC.

Published by Riverbend Books
An Imprint of Bookhouse Group, Inc.
818 Marietta Street, NW
Atlanta, Georgia 30318

www.riverbendbooks.net

(404) 885-9515

ISBN: 1-883987-17-2

SOMETHING'S ALWAYS COOKING at the Frontier. Located across the street from the University of New Mexico and open twenty-four hours a day, many students and area residents begin and end their day at this bustling eatery. Larry and Dorothy Rainosek, who opened the restaurant in 1971, attribute the Frontier's popularity to its friendly atmosphere, rich local color, and delicious food, including Golden Pride barbeque and gigantic, piping hot cinnamon rolls.

Rod Reilly

RUNNING BETWEEN ALAMEDA AND CENTRAL AVENUE,
the two-mile asphalt trail that parallels the Rio Grande attracts
bikers, rollerbladers, runners and strollers year round. The Rio
Grande Nature Center also maintains offshoot trails for nature
and bird walks.

9   *Foreword*

10   *ALBUQUERQUE - Blazing New Trails*

231 *Featured Companies*

238 *Editorial Team*

Chuck Young

ALBUQUERQUE
BLAZING NEW TRAILS

WOULD NOT HAVE BEEN POSSIBLE
WITHOUT THE SUPPORT
OF THE FOLLOWING MAJOR COMPANIES

ALBUQUERQUE
HISPANO
CHAMBER OF COMMERCE

A personal commitment
to New Mexico

TriCore
REFERENCE LABORATORIES

1ST **FIRST STATE BANK**

HEART HOSPITAL
of NEW MEXICO

Burt & Nagel, CPA's
CERTIFIED PUBLIC ACCOUNTANTS
A Limited Liability Company

Downtown Action Team

Business
Improvement District

Eye Associates
of New Mexico

EB
Enterprise Builders
CORPORATION
General Contractor License • #29031

Roses Southwest Papers, Inc.
Tissue, Towel & Bag Converters
Wholesales & Exporters

PRESBYTERIAN

FOREWORD

Growing up in Albuquerque, I've been fortunate to see all of the wonderful changes that have occurred throughout the years. Most recently, the revitalization of downtown, the influx of technology and other industry companies, the positive changes to education, tax policy and economic development and the conscious policy decisions and residents' personal efforts to value the desert's most valuable resource—water. Albuquerque has made a name for itself and each year, the Duke City adds another accolade that heightens its place on the map.

Visitors to Albuquerque are often mesmerized by the beautiful landscape—the majestic purple mountains that residents know and love, the plush, green emanating from the Rio Grande Valley along the river and the high desert foliage that's treasured and respected. Albuquerque boasts some of the most beautiful sunsets ever seen— sunsets that follow the glorious days of sunshine and crystal clear blue skies. At about 310 sun-shining days in the Land of Enchantment, it's no wonder that people from coast to coast make Albuquerque their new home year after year.

The face of the city, both physically and literally, has evolved over the years while maintaining the integrity of what's important to Albuquerque residents. Family plays a tremendous role in the lives of our residents despite culture or background. The family-first attitude has elevated Albuquerque's attractiveness to those looking to escape to a modern, first-class city while still enjoying the precious things in life.

Often, when you live in a place that has so much culture, diversity, physical attraction and quality of life, you tend to overlook the obvious treasures that a city offers. But Albuquerqueans, with their friendliest smiles and cordial ways, will be the first to remind residents and visitors alike of the qualities of this fair city. Whether you're looking to stroll through Old Town, hike or ski at one of the mountain lodges, enjoy a meal at a local restaurant or catch a baseball game, Albuquerque appeals to the masses. And let's not forget our world-renowned Albuquerque International Balloon Fiesta that's held each October. It's an experience that must be felt to fully appreciate and an event that helps drive our local tourism industry.

The economy in Albuquerque continues to boom each year as we're consistently ranked as one of the best cities for companies to relocate. Construction, technology, government, specifically Kirtland Air Force Base and the University of New Mexico, manufacturing, healthcare and hospitality top our city's list of growing industries.

And most recently, the film industry has blossomed and Albuquerque and New Mexico are becoming the backdrops to a good number of movies—look out, the next movie you see might have been shot in our city or state. Albuquerque's increasingly business-friendly climate has also encouraged an emergence of small businesses. And, as in the nation, small businesses are the backbone of any economy, including ours. We're a city to be watched!

Historically, Albuquerque started out as a draw for those who suffered respiratory ailments, and who sought refuge in a dry, sun-filled climate. Today, we continue to be a draw, but for much more than solace from respiratory illnesses. As we further develop as a globally competitive economic region, we maintain the quality of life that makes life worth living.

Albuquerque—Blazing New Trails tells the story of Albuquerque through pictures and words. You'll see the history of the city inter-twined with its modern, present-day feel. We hope you'll enjoy it. Whether you're a native, new to the area or considering a move to the Duke City, you'll be amazed at what you'll see. Enjoy.

-TERRI L. COLE, PRESIDENT & CEO,
GREATER ALBUQUERQUE CHAMBER OF COMMERCE

ALBUQUERQUE'S CLEAN AIR AND EXPANSIVE SKIES make for spectacular sunsets, especially over the surrounding high desert. Far from barren, this desert teems with life, nurturing species both beautiful and hardy, like these spiky-topped Yucca, whose blooms are New Mexico's official state flower.

John Nugent

CHILDREN OF ALL AGES ENJOY STROLLING through the giant pumpkin, one of the many larger-than-life plants and insects in the Children's Fantasy Garden at the Rio Grande Botanic Gardens. Designed to teach visitors about the importance of horticulture, the Botanic Gardens also features a butterfly pavilion and desert and Mediterranean plant conservatories.

Charles Ledford

OPULENT MOVIE HOUSES WERE ALL THE RAGE in the 1920s during Hollywood's most glamorous era and local merchant Oreste Bachechi dreamed of building one in downtown Albuquerque to outshine them all. Designed by Kansas City architect Carl Boller and completed in 1927, the resulting KiMo Theatre incorporated Pueblo Indian motifs, Navajo imagery, western folklore, and American Art Deco into a unique style that would become known as Pueblo Deco. Purchased by the City of Albuquerque in 1977 and lovingly restored over the next several decades, the KiMo (which means "king of its kind" in the Tiwa Indian language) has been returned to its former glory and now serves as a seven-hundred-seat community arts center.

Chuck Young

ALTHOUGH ROBERT GAGNE has served as both a crewmember and passenger during his ten trips to the Albuquerque International Balloon Fiesta, he most enjoys early morning strolls among the balloonists and booth owners. The Fallbrook, California, native is an avid collector of balloon fiesta pins, having filled a jacket, vest, and cowboy hat with over five hundred of the colorful mementos.

Tim Wright

TriCore Reference Laboratories

I f you live in New Mexico, chances are good that your life has been touched by TriCore Reference Laboratories. As a medical testing laboratory serving patients throughout New Mexico as well as parts of Texas, Arizona, Colorado, and Nevada, TriCore provides results that determine diagnosis and treatment for health concerns throughout the region.

TriCore is an independent not-for-profit company formed in 1998 by the consolidation of the medical testing laboratories of the University of New Mexico Hospital, Presbyterian Healthcare Services, and St. Vincent Hospital. Combining these three entities has brought together broad-ranging clinical capabilities, from cholesterol screening to genetics-based diagnostics.

Overcoming the challenges of merging three different healthcare cultures, TriCore staff have become internally aligned toward a common goal—to provide the most accurate results in the timeliest manner. At the core of that customer-driven commitment is a sense of teamwork. "In orientation we tell all new employees to treat patient samples as if they belonged to their loved ones," says President and Chief Executive Officer Russell W. Duke, Ph.D. "We want to make sure everyone understands that what they do is important, because if any one of the one hundred people who may touch a sample before the result is delivered does not do his or her job appropriately, then what the other ninety-nine do is for naught."

TriCore recently relocated to the company's brand-new, state-of-the-art headquarters laboratory in Albuquerque. The 95,000-square-foot facility is at 1001 Woodward Place NE. Architectural services for the laboratory were provided by Dekker/Perich/Sabatini; Flintco Constructive Solutions West was the general contractor.

Pathologist Janet Griego, M.D. (center), and pathology assistants review a surgical biopsy at a multi-headed microscope. TriCore evaluates the biopsy specimen while the patient is still under anesthesia to assist the surgeon with diagnosis and care of the patient.

professionals are not only attuned to advances in their various disciplines, they also participate in research and development of both new and improved testing in facilities such as TriCore's Genetics and Cytometry Laboratory. In addition, the team keeps its skills sharp by working closely with the University of New Mexico Health Sciences Center and other teaching institutions to facilitate clinical pathology rotations and train future laboratory professionals.

continued on page 20

With great attention to convenience for customers, TriCore offers some fifteen patient service centers throughout the Southwest, a statewide courier network, and the availability of interfaced and Internet-based results reporting. TriCore is also able to file claims with hundreds of commercial carriers through its provider participation agreements with local and national insurance companies.

In the ever-evolving field of medical testing, TriCore maintains a leading edge by employing a team of highly trained physicians, scientists, and technologists. These

Medical laboratory technician Martin Leon checks test values to determine the levels of chemicals such as cholesterol, triglycerides, and glucose in the patient's blood.

Charles Ledford — Both

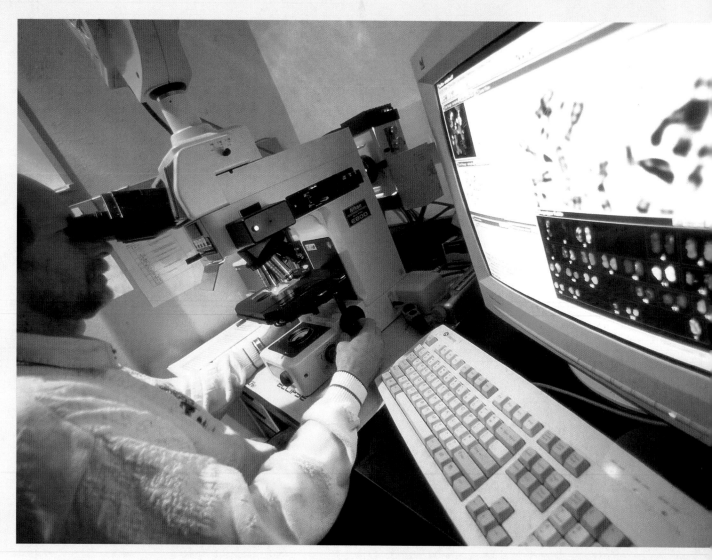

Using a technique called 'spectral karyotyping,' or SKY, Bryan Hall of TriCore's Genetics and Cytometry Laboratory reviews cell chromosomes that have been marked with special stains useful for identifying abnormalities. The SKY technique, a highly specialized form of 'fluorescence in situ hybridization,' or FISH, is but one of the advanced methods TriCore uses to diagnose, monitor and treat disease.

continued from page 19

"We also stay current by constantly looking at better ways of doing things to produce more specific and accurate results," says Duke. "The impact of the mapping of the human genome has had tremendous impact on the laboratory profession. In the future, the greatest innovation we will see is assisting physicians with the application of this tremendous amount of information."

Innovative thinking is another factor responsible for bringing TriCore to its current place as leader in the state's medical testing arena. "The laboratory industry represents about 5 percent of the overall expense in health care, but the information we produce is used in 65 to 70 percent of diagnosis and treatment by physicians," explains Duke. "The economic reality that we may not be receiving our full share of resources for our value has forced us to be innovative." For example, beyond patient-results testing, TriCore generates revenue by supporting clinical and scientific research for the University of New Mexico as well as biotech firms across the nation. The company also earns income by partnering with national vendors to test equipment and provide performance reviews.

TriCore's interest in a healthy community includes substantial contributions of time and funding to support local healthcare-related organizations. "Part of our responsibility is to set the example for leading an intentional

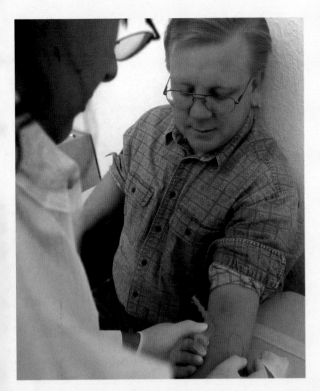

Phlebotomist Juanita Baca draws blood from Shayne Moreshead. TriCore operates patient centers throughout New Mexico and the region, offering patients the ability to choose a location convenient to where they live or work.

'corporate' life," says Stella Saindon, TriCore's chief financial officer. "Participating in activities that make Albuquerque a better place to live is part of that effort."

"Today a successful corporation is not all about profits," Duke agrees. "You must balance having a conscience and caring about the good of your customers, employees, and your community. TriCore believes that it is everyone's responsibility to make the community better—and since our employees live and prosper in Albuquerque, we encourage them to be involved as well. Those businesses that care and are involved will have long-term sustainability."

With plans to double in size that include the recently completed expansion of physical property, and increases in personnel numbers, market share, and service area, TriCore is certain to thrive in the days to come. And as it rises to join the ranks of the nation's largest medical laboratories, TriCore will surely bring even greater prosperity to the community it calls home. ◆

Rebecca Smith of TriCore's Microbiology/Virology Department analyzes DNA for bacterial strain identification.

Charles Ledford — All

SEVERAL TIMES EACH YEAR IN FALL, the dark skies over Albuquerque are lit up by something other than stars. Those times occur during balloon fiesta, with the eagerly anticipated Special Shapes Glowdeo and the spectacular *Albuquerque Journal*-sponsored AfterGlow fireworks show that follows.

Tim Wright

Burt & Nagel, CPA's, LLC

For Burt & Nagel, CPA's, LLC, what really counts is using industry expertise to enhance the quality of life for the people of Albuquerque. From structural reorganization to employee benefit packages, Burt & Nagel has helped entrepreneurs Jean and Mark Bernstein mold their Flying Star Cafes into an enterprise capable of measuring itself against national restaurant chains.

"We look at Burt & Nagel as one of our strategic partners," says Flying Star Controller Donna Schmidt. "We find it helpful to have an outside opinion and they are really good at focusing on the bigger picture." Today, this chain of eight restaurants and coffee shops provides delectable menu options for paying customers and is a staple contributor to charitable activities that feed members of the community in need.

A visual display of community spirit is a key to success for Charles "Chick" Hancock, owner of Chick's Harley-Davidson/Buell. A former banker, Hancock turned around a struggling dealership by using a disciplined business approach that began with participation in activities that were highly visible to a new segment of clientele. "The key thing in changing the image was to be the good guys," he says, "so we did some really high profile charity events." It is a business practice that makes both financial and philosophical sense. "It's the best publicity you can get," says Hancock, "but it's also something that was a constant message to me growing up—that money isn't everything, you have to do the right thing." For Hancock, doing the right thing also meant turning to Burt & Nagel for help, and by taking the firm's advice on matters ranging from auditing and accounting to personnel placement and benefits. Since then, Hancock's operation has become more operationally self-sufficient and expanded tenfold in size.

As a member of the Board of Elders of Heights Christian Church, Burt & Nagel Managing Director Roger Nagel helps provide quality daycare for Albuquerque families by using his knowledge of business management principles to help shape the organization's future.

Tim Wright—All

(l-r) Burt & Nagel Senior Member Dennis Burt with David Daniell and Gary Mallory, owners of Heads Up Landscape Contractors. Over the years, Burt & Nagel consulting has helped Heads Up grow from a small sprinkler installation company to one of the nation's largest residential and commercial landscaping contractors.

Up President Gary Mallory, who was hesitant but surprised by the experience. "And I would never made that next step, this wonderful part in evolving my business knowledge, without their suggestion." Today, Heads Up Landscaping is one of the nation's largest landscapers, employing some 150 personnel.

continued on page 26

To see the dedication of Burt & Nagel, one only need look around the Albuquerque landscape. This beautiful city is, in part, a product of the firm's twenty-five year relationship with Gary Mallory and David Daniell, owners of Heads Up Landscape Contractors. As a trusted business advisor, the firm provided strategic mentoring and reorganization services, ultimately reaching its skill limitations and recommending peer involvement for the company. "I almost immediately had access to the most successful people in the industry," says Heads

Dennis Burt with clients Mark and Jean Bernstein, owners of Flying Star Cafes, a growing local restaurant chain named one of *Bon Appetit* magazine's 10 Favorite Places for Breakfast in America.

continued from page 25

Simultaneously, a quarter century ago, Heights Christian Church was just beginning a program to provide a day out for mothers. Today, that program is one of Albuquerque's most highly respected day-care centers, providing quality care for over one hundred families. Burt & Nagel volunteerism has provided guidance for this program, exploring the potential for an infant care program connected with a local pregnancy crisis counseling center. Senior Pastor Don Kimbro explains one reason for the expansion of services. "We believe in the importance of the American family," he says. "And if we can offer services that will help keep families together and make them stronger, we believe that will have a great impact on our society and community." That same impact is what Burt & Nagel, CPA's, LLC, strives for in its effort to serve every member of the Albuquerque community. ◆

(l-r) Chick Hancock and Roger Nagel at Chick's Harley-Davidson/Buell, working together and enjoying the ride while raising funds for firemen. Community spirit is a thriving part of business practices for both of these local leaders.

Burt & Nagel, CPA's
CERTIFIED PUBLIC ACCOUNTANTS
A Limited Liability Company

INCLUDED IN THE CITY OF ALBUQUERQUE'S EXTENSIVE COLLECTION of publicly owned art are these two life-size bronze figures, part of Santa Fe artist Glenna Goodacre's ten-figure "Sidewalk Society" sculpture, located downtown at Third Street and Tijeras. Established in 1978, Albuquerque's Public Art Program is funded in part by an ordinance that sets aside 1 percent of revenues from the general obligation bond.

John Nugent

Goodwill Industries of New Mexico

Whenever someone clears out a closet, garage, or kitchen cabinet, Goodwill Industries of New Mexico stands to open a door of opportunity. That is because Goodwill sells gently used items to help local residents overcome barriers to employment.

From shoes and suits to fry pans and furniture to balls and bats, Goodwill Industries of New Mexico welcomes donations of materials that can be resold as merchandise in any of its many stores around the state. The revenue derived from the sale of these items, along with monetary donations, is then used to fund employment and training programs that help people whose physical or economic circumstances prevent them from working.

Dale was one of these people. Born with a learning disability, Dale found employment with an auto dealership after completing Goodwill's job skills training program in the mid-1990s. Four years later, Dale had the skills and the confidence to secure a position of greater responsibility at a high technology company. Today, Dale is living on his own and pursuing a lead position that will give him the opportunity to train other individuals.

Because of changing times, Goodwill no longer repairs most items, but its wonderful donors ensure that only quality items reach its store shelves. The organization has earned its place in bargain hunters' hearts, and in fact, is gaining attention for its innovative online site, www.shopgoodwill.com. Among the myriad of annual donations it receives, Goodwill discovers absolute treasures such as antiques, artwork, and fine jewelry. These items go online and are auctioned, but still make up a small fraction of donations-so that the retail stores maintain their share of fabulous

Having completed the intensive Retail Skills Training Program, Goodwill Industries of New Mexico's Graduate of the Year Debbie Brown (l) discusses her new position at Macy's West in Coronado Mall with Wanda Easley Small, Human Resources Manager for Macy's.

Chuck Young—Both

items. In the meantime, Goodwill has further enhanced its online shopping options with a web-based company store that offers new merchandise, with or without the Goodwill logo.

Goodwill Industries excels by providing opportunities for individuals whose working lives are halted by barriers. Doris is just one individual who had been helped by Goodwill's Retail Skills Training Program. A single parent, Doris struggled to stay employed because she often lacked the proper childcare, attire, and transportation, but three days after graduation from the program, Doris found her niche as a

Retail Sales Associate. Don is another example of Goodwill's retail training success. When disease caused him to lose the function in his arm and subsequently become unemployed after twenty years in retail, Don found himself relearning skills that had once come naturally to him. Today, Don has returned to employment.

Every year, Goodwill Industries of New Mexico serves over one thousand individuals like Dale, Doris, and Don. Through its training programs and placement services, Goodwill helps people not only gain self esteem, but also become self sufficient members of society. ◆

SAN FELIPE DE NERI CATHOLIC CHURCH, whose Spanish Colonial facade overlooks Old Town Plaza, has been in continual operation since it was built in 1793. The church is open to the public daily, with English and Spanish mass held several times during the weekend and at special times at Christmas and Easter.

AN OPEN-MINDED AND MULTI-CULTURAL CITY, Albuquerque supports many religious faiths. While Roman Catholics are most predominant, others, such as this Greek Orthodox monk, happily call the city home as well.

John Nugent

ALBUQUERQUE'S VALLEY NEIGHBORHOODS house many families whose history in the area goes back for generations. Gerry Marsico's grandparents first settled in the south valley at the turn of the twentieth century. She and her husband Don still live there, in the house they built on Gerry's family land in 1953. Their legacy includes two sons, one of whom lives across the street, and six grandchildren.

Rod Reilly

Citibank

Looking back over their twenty-year history in Albuquerque, Citibank can point with pride to the various ways in which their motto "Live Richly" has benefitted their employees, their customers, and their community.

As a member of Citigroup, the largest financial services company in the world, Citibank has grown to over fifty million credit card members served by corporate offices worldwide, offices built on strong local foundations.

Here in Albuquerque, Citibank's foundation rests on the partnership environment it has established with its employees. As one of the city's top private employers Citibank fosters and supports a diverse workforce by providing on-going training, competitive compensation, and outstanding benefits. As a result, Albuquerque's 1,300-person call center boasts one of the lowest turnover rates in the industry.

Citibank encourages their customers to live richly by maintaining a healthy balance between financial concerns and overall quality of life. Behind every cardholder is a person with unique financial needs and Citibank addresses those needs with personalized services such as credit card payment plans, twenty-four-hour customer service, and top-notch financial services products.

Citibank's motto even takes on a physical form. In addition to volunteering time and money to a variety of programs, each year Citibank participates directly in the Habitat for Humanity program. Hundreds of Citibank employees chip in to help build a house for one of Albuquerque's needy families, proving that volunteerism is one of the company's richest resources. ◆

How does one become the leading credit card issuer in the world today? By providing twenty-four-hour, seven-day-a-week customer support in the form of well-trained and enthusiastic employees. The Albuquerque call center alone employs 1,300 staffers.

Chuck Young

TANGO PASION is just one of the many exciting yearly events at Popejoy Hall, the University of New Mexico's premier performing arts venue. Performed entirely through dance and music, *Tango Pasion* is choreographed by Argentinean ballet master Hector Zaraspe and orchestrated by Sexteto Mayor, considered by many critics to be the best tango orchestra in the world.

Charles Ledford

Gap Inc.

Gap Inc. was founded in 1969 by Donald and Doris Fisher in San Francisco, California, with a single store and a handful of employees. Today, the company is one of the world's largest specialty retailers with nearly 4,300 stores and 165,000 employees supporting three of the most recognized and respected brands in the apparel industry—Gap, Banana Republic, and Old Navy.

Gap Inc. relies on its Albuquerque-based Corporate Shared Services Center (CSSC), established in June 2001, for financial and human resources services that help keep its domestic and global operations running efficiently.

"Our role is to support the company's employees around the world with excellent customer service and operational efficiency," says Brandy Sanders, director of human resources. "The better service we provide to our store employees, the quicker they can get back to their jobs of providing excellent customer service to Gap Inc.'s customers."

The CSSC has developed into a valuable support network for the community as well. Most of its 315 employees were recruited locally and the center relies heavily on TVI and UNM's Anderson School of Management Business School for entry-level professional placement.

Likewise, volunteerism is strongly encouraged and rewarded. Each volunteer hour completed by an employee on his or her own time is matched by paid time to volunteer during work hours, making it possible for employees to participate in community activities such as the NM AIDs Walk, Mudd Volleyball for Carrie Tingley Hospital, the Humane Society's Doggie Dash and Dawdle, and Coats for Kids. ◆

Gap Inc.'s employees are a talented and diverse group of individuals who are given exciting opportunities to learn, stretch and grow.

John Nugent

FIRST BUILT IN 1966, THE INTERSTATES 40 AND 25 INTERCHANGE was designed to handle only sixty thousand cars per day. By the New Millennium, the Big I, as it's known locally, was completely outdated. Rebuilt in only two years, the new interchange stands as a marvel of civil engineering, with eight flyover bridges that guide over three-hundred thousand commuters through the city each day. Local company Twin Mountain Construction served as lead contractor on the Big I rebuild. By implementing innovative techniques and a twenty-four-hour-a-day schedule, Twin Mountain president Van Groves (shown here) brought the project in under budget and under schedule with zero loss time due to accidents. The company won a national award for construction excellence.

Charles Ledford

ALBUQUERQUE NATIVE AND WORLD-RENOWNED ARCHITECT Bart Prince designs from what he calls the "inside out"—applying his unique perspective and knowledge of light, space and materials to create buildings that are as much about his clients' needs as they are about his vision. Here, he poses in front of his own home, located at Marquette and Buena Vista, with one of his current projects, a vacation residence for a client in Datil, New Mexico.

Rod Reilly

First State Bank

While First State Bank delivers all the same products as other banks, what makes this company unique is its method of delivery. "We are not your typical bankers, not your typical bank," says President and Chief Executive Officer Michael R. Stanford. "We provide all the same products that other banks do, but we deliver them with style and great service."

Customers Vic and Joni Brenneisen of Joni's Hallmark Shop in Santa Fe can testify to First State's responsive business culture. After becoming commercial patrons at the urging of a friend on the First State team, the retailers soon found themselves in familiar company. "Being in the retail business, we are extremely concerned about customer service," says Vic Brenneisen. "And since we've been at First State, we've found a professional atmosphere with folks who are extremely helpful and responsive to our needs." At the retailer's simple suggestion, First State made immediate enhancements to drive-through service by improving communication during the transaction.

Keith Mallory, owner of American Escrow, Mallory Realty and Investment, and Mallory Pet Supply, has also found First State's expertise to be a valuable asset. "First State is extremely proactive to the small business environment," he says. "As my businesses have expanded, my needs have increased and changed, and they've been very proactive about coming to see us to offer their products, versus us having to find out that they offered them. As a result, a couple of things that we thought we'd never be able to do, we've done with them." Such considerations led Mallory to consider personal banking options, too. "The bank that I was dealing with was bought out and became very impersonal to me

Believing that business is best conducted "from the inside out," dedicated personnel work to guarantee dedicated customers. No matter the size or type of transaction, First State employees make it their goal to out-service the competition.

Alan Weiner—All

after me being there for quite a long time," he says. "The way they treated me at First State made me want to take my personal accounts there as well."

Indeed, dedicated personnel can be considered the bank's finest asset. "We conduct business from the inside out," says Stanford. "Our employees are some of our happiest customers, and with their support and belief in the bank, we are able to out-service the competition. That's the central explanation for our success and why our customers choose us over the competition."

First State's treatment of individual account holders has earned it the loyalty of long-time residents like Crystal Crockett, who prefers banking with familiar faces. "I know everybody there and everybody knows me," she says of her favorite neighborhood branch. From cashing a check to tracking payments, Crockett knows she can rely on assistance from the people at First State. "They're very courteous people, very nice, and they always step up and help me if I have questions or problems," she says. "That's why I'm there, and I'll always be there."

continued on page 42

Not your typical bankers; not your typical bank building. Like this one on Wyoming and Academy, First State Bank branches are easily recognizable by their distinct New Mexican architecture.

continued from page 41

Beyond the business of banking, First State also responds to community needs, providing monetary support, leadership, and hands-on help to local organizations that benefit various segments of the population. "We want the community and the state to be as successful as possible, and if we can help in achieving success, we'll pitch in wherever we're needed," explains Stanford. Participation in activities that benefit homeowners, youth, and persons with special needs characterize more than a corporation with conscience, they illustrate First State Bank's understanding that its success is integrally tied to the strength of its community. ◆

With over sixteen conveniently located ATMs throughout the city, First State Bank customers can access their accounts any time, day or night, at no extra charge.

FOR TWO WEEKS EACH SEPTEMBER a million plus visitors flock to Albuquerque for the New Mexico State Fair, the largest of its kind in the United States. The fair's famous midway is definitely the place for thrill seekers to test their mettle and their stomachs with gravity-defying rides like the Mega Drop. This European-designed ride relies on state-of-the-art hydraulics and old-fashioned physics to send riders racing towards the ground from 135 feet in the air.

John Nugent

John Nugent

THE NEW MEXICO STATE FAIR TAPS ALL YOUR SENSES, ranging from the sights and sounds of the raucous and neon-colored midway, filled with amusement park rides and carnival booths, to food courts boasting tasty treats to fit any set of taste buds. Here, that means everything from staples like cotton candy, turkey legs, and curly fries to local favorites like burritos, Indian fry bread, and Mexican-style fruit drinks.

AWARDED BEST BED AND BREAKFAST by the New Mexico Hotel and Motel Association, the Bottger Mansion is a favorite with visitors looking for something special. Built as a private residence in 1912, the owners began to house travelers during the Roaring Twenties, when Machine Gun Kelly and his gang were frequent guests. Today, the Bottger Mansion is an elegant Victorian-style bed and breakfast noted for gracious hospitality and luxurious accommodations. The pink and white American Foursquare-style building is also the only lodging available within historic Old Town proper, putting it within walking distance of many area attractions.

Alan Weiner — Both

Bank of America

Consider the comfort of dealing with a bank that employs a staff of local people who believe in providing exceptional service and where products and prices are convenient and competitively priced. This is Bank of America, a place where everyone accepts responsibility (and has the power) to do the right thing for clients and customers. A bank whose people enthusiastically support the entire Albuquerque community: local schools, youth programs, the arts, health and human services, community development, and the underserved.

Indeed, it is a neighborhood institution with integrity, character, and a long history of serving its local business partners, friends, and neighbors.

Now, consider the even greater satisfaction that comes from knowing your bank also provides you with choice, convenience, and coast-to-coast access of nationwide banking. That support is provided by thousands of offices, ATMs, and products and services facilities in twenty-one states. All this constitutes a banking company of such size and scope that it can (and does) spend almost $3 billion a year on technology alone—a visionary investment that lets you bank how and when you want, by phone and computer anywhere in the world.

At Bank of America, we bring with us the people and the technology to create new possibilities and new solutions. And we have the spirit and compassion to contribute to the futures of the communities we serve. ◆

Bank of America has committed to improving the lives of people in our communities. Associates like these, pictured at a recent Habitat for Humanity project in Albuquerque, volunteer hundreds of hours to schools, churches, and not-for-profit organizations across the franchise.

John Nugent

ALBUQUERQUE WAS SETTLED IN 1706 as a farming village and military outpost, following the traditional Spanish design of a church, homes, and other buildings surrounding a central plaza. The plaza and church still serve their original purpose, but the centuries-old homes and other buildings have been converted into shops, restaurants and art galleries, making Old Town Albuquerque one of the city's most popular attractions.

Charles Ledford

Bank of Albuquerque

In an era of one-size-fits-all banking, Bank of Albuquerque stands out for its commitment to individualized service. Albuquerque's market is made up primarily of privately held and family owned businesses whose needs and concerns differ greatly from those that are investor-based. Bank of Albuquerque meets those needs by tailoring financial solutions to each individual client.

"We consciously resist the trend of taking away decision making authority at the local level that is occurring with large banks throughout the country," says Chairman and CEO Greg Symons. "What differentiates us is the understanding of our local market."

In doing so, Bank of Albuquerque fills a unique niche in its industry. Local banks provide great service but can have limited access to products. Big banks have good products and technology, but their approach to clients is often centralized and impersonal. "But we try to convey something different," says President Paul Sowards. "We deliver world-class products and technology in a manner more indicative of a local, community bank." Consumer bank clients receive the same personalized care, with friendly, professional service and easy access via numerous ATMs, 24-Hour ExpressBank telephone bankers, and on-line services.

This autonomy is both supported and encouraged by the bank's local board of directors and by its principle owner, a successful oil and gas entrepreneur, who is dedicated to the idea that localized customer service is

Bank of Albuquerque's main branch occupies the fourteenth floor of one of the city's most recognizable architectural silhouettes: the twenty-story Hyatt Regency Hotel located in the heart of downtown Albuquerque.

Chuck Young—Both

addition to eighteen conveniently located ranches, Albuquerque residents may also take dvantage of full-service, seven-day-a-week anking at three Albertson's supermarket locations.

the key to success in the banking industry. "People are concerned about the stability of ownership in banking," says Symons. "But this individual is completely dedicated to maintaining his long-term ownership, thus preserving this type of organization."

Established in 1998, Bank of Albuquerque has grown to eighteen branches, is ranked fourth in its market, and is one of Albuquerque's most desirable places to work. Many associated with the bank are either native New Mexican or have ties to the state going back for years.

Symons was born in Colorado but received his MBA from University of New Mexico and played football for the Lobos. Sowards has lived in Albuquerque for fifteen years and accepted the presidency three years ago because, "The bank is in this market because they chose to be in New Mexico. So often banks have a presence in New Mexico only because the state connects Texas to Arizona, or a New Mexico presence is part of a package deal. I want to be associated with an organization that wants to be here, and has a commitment to the employees, clients, and communities in which we do business."

Keeping in mind that a business is only as vibrant as its community, Bank of Albuquerque contributes widely to a variety of programs and organizations that promote economic development, education, and the arts, both in Albuquerque and throughout the state.

"Our three constituencies are our customers, our employees, and our community," says Symons. "Our goals are to be the most respected financial institution within our market, to have our employees think there's no better place to work, and to have our community think the same thing. We want to be seen as a leader, someone to be counted on through thick and thin, someone to do the hard work to make our community a better place to live." ◆

FOUR-YEAR-OLD ADAM BESSEY leads his parents through the Maize Maze, a three-mile labyrinth of paths hand cut into an eight-acre cornfield at Los Poblanos Open Space near the river. A project of Rio Grande Community Farms, the corn maze is cut into a different animal each fall, providing visitors with a fun problem-solving activity and lessons in sustainable agriculture, wildlife habitat, and the history of regional foods.

Tim Wright — Both

NEW MEXICANS LOVE THEIR CORN almost as much as they love their chile. The rich soils of the Rio Grande Valley where Community Farms is located are especially conducive to growing corn and other tasty produce. Once the season ends, corn from the Maize Maze is felled and left as food for visiting Sandhill cranes.

Wells Fargo

On a trip to the West in 1853, Henry Wells was heard to exclaim, "This is a great country, and a greater people!" It was a trip made only one year after Wells, William G. Fargo, and others had formed Wells, Fargo & Company, to provide banking and business express services in California. Since then, Wells Fargo has remained an integral part of making this a great country in which to live, work, and play.

In the years following its founding, Wells Fargo built a reputation for reliability as it hurried express across the nation via stagecoaches, railroads, and steamships. By 1918, a dozen original offices had grown to ten thousand sites nationwide. Wells Fargo & Company is a diversified financial services company with $370 billion in assets, providing banking, insurance, wealth management and estate planning, investments, mortgage and consumer finance from 5,800 stores and the Internet (www.wellsfargo.com) across North America and elsewhere internationally.

A part of the New Mexico landscape since 1882, Wells Fargo has both an historical connection and a deep commitment to building strong communities. Its heritage throughout the state is one of providing high quality financial services, staffing offices with friendly and knowledgeable personnel, and contributing to community endeavors.

With more than one hundred locations, Wells Fargo has grown into New Mexico's largest financial services provider. Still, Wells Fargo remains a community bank, responding to the individual needs of customers with local attention and decision-making. This localized service, combined with an array of individual and business banking

Customers like Luis Herrera (center) appreciate the localized, individualized attention they receive from Wells Fargo team members (top, left to right) Alberto Peralta, Darin Davis, George Sanchez, Becky Shaum, Anthony Justice, Penny Perrigo, and (bottom, left to right) Betty Garcia, Denise Emerson, Loretta Van Paris, and Patty Bergin.

Tim Wright—Both

As owner of the largest corporate balloon division in the country, and one of the largest sponsors of the Albuquerque International Balloon Fiesta, Wells Fargo's dedication to community is vividly portrayed in the skies over New Mexico.

solutions, gives Wells Fargo the resources to fuel growth and prosperity in New Mexico.

Wells Fargo's significant impact on New Mexico can be seen in its brightly lit downtown Albuquerque headquarters building as well as its popular Stagecoach, Miss Penny, and Li'l Buck hot air balloons. From a single balloon, A Loan at Last, purchased in 1987, Wells Fargo has expanded its fleet to a half dozen teardrop and specialty shapes. These bright wonders, comprising one of the largest corporate hot air

balloon divisions in the nation, are stunning entries dotting the sky during the annual Albuquerque International Balloon Fiesta.

In addition to participating in a variety of community and statewide sponsorships, Wells Fargo strongly believes in the power of people working together for the common good—a philanthropic strategy that relies on the local knowledge of team members who live and work in their communities. Through the insight of these dedicated individuals, Wells Fargo is able to provide the funding, volunteer leadership, and strategic planning initiatives that make a difference in areas like economic development, education, healthcare, human services, arts, recreation, and culture.

From building a solid reputation for dependability to building strong communities with quality financial services and involvement, Wells Fargo is—and continues to be—a fundamental participant in making this a great nation. ◆

DURING THE SUMMER, thousands of youngsters head to the beach. The Beach Waterpark that is, where they indulge in hours of water-soaked fun. Attractions on the fourteen-acre park include a seven-hundred-thousand-gallon wave pool, a quarter-mile "Lazy River" tube ride, a children's play area, two inner-tube slides and five body slides.

John Nugent

The University of New Mexico

I t seems everywhere you look in this state there is dynamic evidence of the influence of the University of New Mexico (UNM). Graduates of UNM are leaders of government and industry. Its programs guide advances in the state's health care and technology, its workforce initiatives open doors for both professionals and entry level workers, and its community service activities, as well as its premier cultural and athletic venues, enhance the overall quality of life for the people of this state.

As such an integral part of New Mexico, UNM plays a vital role in the state's economic activity. As well as being a major employer in the state, its graduates account for large percentages of the state's professionals, and many of them are business leaders creating innumerable additional job opportunities as well.

UNM's research activities also support economic vitality, attracting millions of funding dollars that are injected back into the region in the form of job creation, knowledge expansion, technology commercialization and business growth. Among its research success stories, the University counts more than 250 patent cases and 30 licenses and spin-offs. Its research of specific ethnic and regional health issues is providing answers for global concerns. And UNM's collaborations with both public and private entities are creating opportunities for new and existing businesses while developing avenues for technology transfer through its Science and Technology Corporation and its research park.

Lobo athletics draw fans from far and wide, making these games the top sports programs in the state. The more than 18,000-seat University Arena, affectionately known as "The Pit," was ranked among the top twenty sports venues in the nation by *Sports Illustrated* magazine.

John Nugent

Dane Smith Hall is equipped with state-of-the-art classrooms that provide students with access to the latest technology for study in a range of subjects. The UNM campus is an appealing blend of cultural beauty and advanced learning.

A large portion of UNM's student population reflects New Mexico's Hispanic and American Indian populations, fostering the study of regionally specific issues ranging from language and culture to law and water resources. Some of the country's finest fields of study are part of the UNM curriculum and include the School of Medicine, which is ranked a U.S. News and World

continued on page 60

But perhaps UNM's greatest contributions are the more than four thousand graduates who enter the world each year, equipped with the values, skills and knowledge to be part of their growing communities. On an annual basis, more than thirty thousand students attend UNM's campus and branches around the state, choosing educational paths from more than two hundred degree programs at the baccalaureate, graduate, and professional levels, as well as dozens of certificate programs.

The beauty of UNM's Spanish Pueblo Revival Style architecture is reflected throughout the campus in buildings like University House. Built in 1930 as a home for the presidential family, the building continues to be a residence, dignitary welcome center, and symbol of architectural excellence.

continued from page 59

Report top ten medical school in the areas of primary care, rural medicine, and family medicine. The School of Law is noted for its racial diversity and clinical law training. And the School of Engineering's graduate program is among the top forty in research expenditures in the nation.

UNM's hospital facilities support its health sciences mission, providing some of the region's most comprehensive care in a hands-on learning environment. The UNM Health Sciences Center (HSC) is the state's largest center for integrated health care, research and education, treating more than seven-hundred thousand outpatient cases each year and housing the state's only Level I Trauma Center. At any given time, there are between 450 and 500 medical residents at HSC, rotating through all medical specialties. Within the HSC is UNM Hospital, a highly regarded teaching hospital that through its nursing residency program, provides nurses with comprehensive patient care experience in a clinical setting. The HSC also houses the UNM Children's Hospital and the UNM Cancer Research and Treatment Center, each providing patients with state-of-the-art care and students with world-class learning opportunities. The Carrie Tingley Hospital is also a UNM facility that delivers treatment for the most complex musculoskeletal and orthopedic conditions in children and adolescents.

(l-r): Rita Lovett and Marilyn Rodriguez practice cardiopulmonary resuscitation on "Stan," a computerized human simulator that reacts with lifelike responses to a wide range of life threatening conditions. Stan is used by trainees statewide in a variety of health care fields.

Hundreds of employers from around Albuquerque come to UNM's periodic Continuing Education Job Fairs to talk with students in the program's skills, training, and development II studies.

Charles Ledford—All

Many of these programs are offered through UNM's Division of Continuing Education and Community Service, where each year, tens of thousands of students advance through courses ranging from industry-specific training to welfare-to-work programs to learning just for fun. As New Mexico's leader in lifelong learning, UNM Continuing Education provides high quality training in alternative formats that responds to the needs of both employers and employees. Whether training is in the area of computer and information technology, professional development or language skills, Continuing Education provides customized, on-site training and certificate programs that suit the needs of the area's businesses.

continued on page 62

With institutes and centers like the Bureau of Business and Economic Research on campus, it makes sense that business leaders and government agencies turn to UNM for information and support. To meet the evolving needs of industry, UNM continues to develop a host of workforce training and development programs designed to strengthen the skills of those pursuing careers while improving the efficiency of employed professionals.

Christopher Stearns performs testing in the UNM Health Sciences Center. UNM's research has earned worldwide recognition including title to one of the National Science Foundation's "Nifty 50" discoveries, for detection and treatment of the deadly hantavirus.

continued from page 61

When classroom courses do not fit a busy schedule, the division offers online computer classes that promote professional advancement.

At the core of the UNM mission is its commitment to positive interaction in the community. Whether it is engaging in classroom preparation, partnering with area businesses, providing data to government officials, improving neighborhood amenities, or enriching people's daily lives with cultural and athletic events, UNM students, faculty, and staff know that a healthy community is one where everyone works together. It is this desire-and capability-to reach out beyond the campus that will continue to make the University of New Mexico a vital, dynamic member of the New Mexico community. ♦

Giovanni Donati in the Center for High Technology Materials (CHTM), nationally recognized for its research in the areas of photonics and microelectronics. CHTM is one of UNM's many Research Centers that perform groundbreaking studies on everything from culture and environment to economics and health care.

Charles Ledford

Tim Wri

▲ **OPPORTUNITIES ABOUND FOR SKILLED ATHLETES** of both sexes who attend
Albuquerque Public Schools. Here, Tracy Diver, kicker for the Manzano Monarch's
Junior Varsity football team, waits on the sidelines for her chance to score another
field goal. One of several female kickers in APS athletics, Tracy is an all-around
outstanding athlete, excelling as well in track, soccer, and swimming.

St. Pius X High School

First-time visitors to St. Pius X High School might think they've just stepped onto a college campus. That's because the forty-acre park-like setting of Albuquerque's only Catholic high school occupies the site of the former University of Albuquerque.

Established in 1956 by the Archdiocese of Santa Fe, St. Pius is a private, co-educational school that serves more than one thousand students of all races and faiths in grades nine through twelve. Living up to its motto, "Teach me goodness, discipline, knowledge," St. Pius X has a proven track record of helping students with a wide range of abilities achieve extraordinary performance.

Dr. Mary McLeod, who in July 2000 became St. Pius' first lay principal, attributes the school's success to its core Catholic values that promote moral, spiritual, intellectual, and physical growth. "I think it's important that we work to have a strong Catholic identity," she says. "What we assumed forty or fifty years ago to be part of people's value systems are now getting lost, but we're holding on to those values here."

As a result, academics are not taught in a vacuum. "Because we uphold Jesus Christ as a model for life, we don't talk a lot about careers," Dr. McLeod continues. "Rather we emphasize that students find their vocation, their special talent, for which they have been given to share with others."

Because learning is seen as preparation for life as well as for college, St. Pius students are encouraged to optimize their potential no matter what the final goal. Here, Ashley Roybal and Clint Collier perform an experiment in teacher Kathy Ravano's eleventh-grade chemistry class.

Rod Reilly—Both

believing that a diverse student body creates a lively community and an open-minded approach to learning, St. Pius welcomes students from a variety of economic, religious, and ethnic backgrounds.

Classes are modestly sized and teachers, many of whom hold advanced degrees, are dedicated to a diverse, challenging college preparatory curriculum. To promote cultural awareness, tolerance, self-esteem and a healthy sense of competition, students are also encouraged to participate in the school's esteemed fine arts and athletics programs.

The result is a well-rounded and creative student body ready to take on the challenges of life outside the classroom. Because St. Pius graduates consistently rank high in national exams, many of the 95 percent who continue their education do so on a college or university scholarship.

In addition to maintaining high academic and ethical standards, St. Pius also strives to admit all qualified students, regardless of their ability to pay. To assist with that goal, a concerned group of parents established the St. Pius X High School Foundation in 1986. The purpose of this organization centers around uniting the Catholic and Albuquerque community in support of the school by raising funds for current use, endowment, and capital projects.

Dr. McLeod believes that providing worthy students with a superior education benefits not only the students and their families, but also New Mexico as a whole. "It's how we give back to the community," she says. "A lot of our kids have deep roots in Albuquerque and are from families who have lived here for generations. The core values and quality education students receive at St. Pius X High School prepare them to be future leaders of New Mexico." ◆

COMPRISED OF CHEERLEADERS AND MEMBERS OF THE MAJESTIX DRILL TEAM, the Manzano Monarch's Spirit Squad lends its support to all the school's teams, both at home and on the road. The girls also compete in major regional and national competitions and recently took first in state at the Universal Cheerleaders Association competition.

THE LA CUEVA BEARS beat the Manzano Monarchs 21-14 in this non-district game between two of Albuquerque's top Northeast Heights high schools. Both schools rank among the best in the city for their academic, athletic, and special education programs.

LIKE THE SPIRIT SQUAD, Manzano's Royal Guard marching band plays at every football game. The Royal Guard also performs concerts throughout the school year and competes in regional and national competitions.

Tim Wright — All

THE RIO GRANDE, which meanders north to south through the city, is home to a variety of plants and animals and is a favorite resting stop for migratory birds. Visitors who want to learn more about this fascinating ecosystem begin with a trip to the Rio Grande Nature Center, located where Candelaria dead ends at the river. Open year round, the Center offers a variety of programs to encourage understanding and conservation of the Rio Grande and its Bosque, (a Spanish word referring to the forest of cottonwood trees along the river's banks) including nature walks and bird watching tours.

Chuck Young

Downtown Action Team
& Historic District Improvement Company

H ailed by National Public Radio (NPR) as the "fastest downtown turnaround in the country", Downtown Albuquerque is the talk of the town! In an ambitious 10 year revitalization effort, Downtown has exceeded all expectations.

Downtown Albuquerque is simply unlike any other downtown in the country. Anchored by historic "Route 66," Downtown is an eclectic mix of art, entertainment, history, culture and commerce. By day, Downtown Albuquerque is New Mexico's Downtown – the largest business center in the state, home to the state's largest financial institutions, its top law firms, major corporate headquarters, and government centers.

But Downtown Albuquerque is much, much more! It is here that hip outdoor cafes, first-class restaurants and hotels, exciting and unique entertainment venues, and some of the city's trendiest and most historic places to live all merge to comprise a unique urban experience – one that pays tribute to the past while looking to the future.

Downtown's vibrant, neon-lit Arts & Entertainment District is home to Albuquerque's diverse live music and club scene. Performing arts venues abound in and around Downtown.

Downtown's vibrant, neon-lit Arts & Entertainment District is home to Albuquerque's diverse live music and club scene. Here, patrons enjoy a drink at the bar of O-PM, an exciting dance, live and DJ-spun music scene.

Charles Ledford

Downtown Albuquerque at night is a colorful, neon-lit destination for shoppers, diners, music lovers, and theatergoers.

studios, galleries and art organizations. Downtown also serves as the gateway to a number of unique cultural and historic experiences. Within minutes of Downtown, you can visit Albuquerque's BioPark (encompassing the Rio Grande Zoo, Aquarium and Botanic Gardens),

continued on page 72

You can catch a show at the historic KiMo Theater or at the City's Kiva Auditorium, watch a play at Albuquerque's own Little Theater Playhouse, experience the cultural offerings of the South Broadway Cultural Center, or the spectacular new Roy E. Disney Center for the Performing Arts at the National Hispanic Cultural Center, or see a performance at the edgy Cell Black Box Theatre.

Downtown's emerging Central Arts District – anchored by Magnifico, Albuquerque's urban contemporary arts center and gallery – is fast becoming THE gathering place for artist co-ops,

The main east/west artery through downtown Albuquerque, Central Avenue follows the path of Route 66, America's "Mother Road." In the past, this stretch was dotted with small businesses and motor lodges; today it's part of one of the city's most vibrant residential, retail, and commercial corridors.

Diners like to see and be seen at one of Downtown's most trendy restaurant/bars, Raw, which features the hottest dance tunes, an inventive drink menu and edgy, urban décor.

Alan Weiner

continued from page 71

Historic Old Town and its many museums, the Indian Pueblo Cultural Center and the incredible new National Hispanic Cultural Center.

Whether a first time visitor to Downtown Albuquerque or if you've lived here your entire life, enjoying all Downtown has to offer is easier than ever. In Downtown, the pedestrian – not the car – is king! We've done away with our one-way streets, implemented a new pedestrian-friendly wayfinding system, developed a convenient Park Once system for the motorists, and built a brand new multi-modal Transportation Center to make it much easier for the non-motorists to access Downtown by train, bus or taxi. And if you need directions, an escort to your car or want to find a place to have lunch or dinner, a red-shirted Downtown Ambassador will be there to assist you – with a smile!

The revitalization of Downtown Albuquerque is due in large part to the combined efforts of the Downtown Action Team (DAT) and the Historic District Improvement Company (HDIC). DAT is a private, non-profit organization dedicated to the revitalization of Downtown Albuquerque as the best mid-sized downtown in the USA. Its advocacy for Downtown puts goodwill ambassadors on the streets, provides maintenance and clean services, sponsors

Alan Weiner

The City of Albuquerque and local developer Paradigm & Company teamed up in 2000 to renovate the old Albuquerque High School building at the corner of Central and Broadway. Today, the structure is an attractive retail/residential space featuring shops and loft-style apartments.

Need help or directions when visiting downtown? Just look for the red-jacketed members of the Action Team's Safety Ambassadors who are stationed throughout various areas downtown.

Charles Ledford

entertainment programs and events, and fosters public and private cooperation for quality growth and investment in Downtown development. (505-243-2230; www.downtownabq.com)

HDIC has served as the catalytic developer for Albuquerque's ambitious Downtown revitalization. HDIC is a unique merger of a for-profit development entity (Arcadia Land Company, one of the nation's premier New Urbanist developers), with a not-for-profit charitable foundation (the McCune Charitable Foundation, the largest foundation serving the New Mexico community). The combination has proved remarkable – blending entrepreneurship with community mission. HDIC has pioneered a number of cutting edge initiatives – in both the architectural world and in the world of finance – right here in Downtown Albuquerque. (505-244-9339; www.nmdowntown.com) ◆

A customer peruses the racks at Jack Flash, the latest venture from local retail clothing maven Jackie Gonzales. Located at 317 Gold Street, the boutique features cutting-edge street wear from European designers such as Fornarina and G-star.

Alan Weiner

MAINTAINING THE WORLD'S LONGEST TRAMWAY is no easy task. In addition to his technical know how, Daniel Bunch possesses a steady foot and a head for heights. As a result, each visitor taking the thirty-minute tram ride up Sandia Mountain to its peak is rewarded with a safe and fascinating trip culminating in an eleven thousand-square-mile panoramic view of the city and beyond. When you're finished with the view, you can take in a delightful meal in the restaurant at the top.

SANDIA PEAK

Charles Ledford

Bernalillo County

ernalillo County government has been and continues to be a guiding force for progress in New Mexico. The County is dedicated to a commitment of financial stability, planned growth, and economic development while providing an unsurpassed quality of life for residents. In the course of achieving these goals, partnerships have become a valuable asset. Striving for the most effective methods, the County Commission fosters cooperation between government and the private sector. These partnerships combine resources including skills, labor, and funding, resulting in a proven formula for success.

Beginning its fourth season this spring, the Journal Pavilion was the County's first private/public venture. Sting, Santana, Toby Keith, Bonnie Raitt, and the New Mexico Symphony Orchestra performed for audiences at this unique regional complex. Surrounded by the majestic Sandia Mountains and beautiful star-filled nights, the Pavilion offers a variety of exciting entertainment experiences for thousands of concert fans. Working together, the New Mexico State Land Office, Bernalillo County, and Clear Channel Entertainment have created a venue unsurpassed in the region.

Established in 1989, the East Mountain Inter Agency Fire Protection Association (EMIFPA) is comprised of members from thirteen agencies and organizations. Some of those members, l-r: Bernalillo County Commissioner Alan B. Armijo; Karen Takai, US Forest Service; Dave Bervin, NM State Forestry Clark "Sparkie" Speakman, Sandoval County Fire Dept.; and (on top of truck) Bernalillo County Fire Chief Bett Clark.

John Nugent—Both

Opening in June of 2000, Journal Pavilion has been host to the country's most elite performers and has entertained more than 600,000 fans in its first four years. An outdoor amphitheatre, the pavilion operates from May to June each year.

The ancient "El Camino Real" (Royal Road) and the original Route 66 are just part of the history of Isleta Boulevard. A major arterial located in Bernalillo County, it is undergoing a dramatic transformation. The improvements to Isleta will provide safety and convenience to residents as well as stimulate economic expansion in the area.

Once the reconstruction is complete, the road will be a varying three-lane to five-lane facility including bike trails, lighting, landscaping, and drainage. The County is in charge of design and construction, but the realization of the project is due to a multi-agency partnership. Funds and support have come from the Metropolitan Transportation Board, the New Mexico Congressional Delegation, the New Mexico Legislature, and Albuquerque Metropolitan Flood Control Authority. The community supported the project by approving bonds and offering input during the design and planning phase.

The East Mountain Area of Bernalillo County is surrounded by National Forest offering the pristine, quiet beauty of pine trees and foliage; yet residents are constantly facing the possibility of wildfire. The East Mountain Interagency Fire Protection Association, consisting of thirteen separate agencies and organizations, was created after two devastating fires moved quickly through forested areas and subdivisions, requiring multi-agency response. The agencies immediately implemented a proactive approach to future possibilities of wildfire in their urban-wildland interface neighborhoods. The result is a group that is a collaboration of fire and emergency response personnel, neighborhood associations, and non-profit agencies. Through training, education and coordination, these organizations can easily become one effective group in the event of a disaster.

These are just a few examples of the many partnerships spearheaded by Bernalillo County. Innovative and advanced, these successful joint efforts push the boundaries of bureaucracy, blazing new trails for progress. ◆

THE DAY MAY BE ENDING BUT THE GAME'S JUST BEGINNING as Jewell Mechanical faces off against Montaño Lath and Plaster, just two teams among dozens who participate each year in the City of Albuquerque Parks and Recreation's adult softball program. Located at Los Altos Park at the corner of Lomas and Eubank, Parks and Rec also has adult programs in tennis, flag football, volleyball, baseball, and basketball.

Tim Wright

THE MILE HIGH LITTLE LEAGUE ROOKIE DIVISION represents about twenty-five out of forty total Little League Teams. Here, the Braves square off against the Diamondbacks for an early season game at Dale Bellamah Park off Juan Tabo and Lomas. Little League season starts in April and continues until mid June. Forming the backbone of Albuquerque Little League are the dozens of coaches who volunteer their time for the love of the game and the love of the kids. Both boys and girls are welcome to play, as are challenged youth, who form their own sixteen-team division.

Rod Reilly — All

THE CORRALES CALYPSO VERSUS the Taylor Ranch Trouble in the Tenth Annual Jamila Himeur Soccer Tournament. Played in honor of the tournament's namesake, a three-year-old who died in 1992 from injuries, the tournament has raised tens of thousands of dollars for various children's charities throughout New Mexico.

John Nuger

PNM
(Public Service Company of New Mexico)

When New Mexicans need energy for their homes and businesses, they know they can rely on their neighbors at PNM.

Founded in 1917, PNM has grown into a company of some 2,600 employees providing electricity and gas services for 1.3 million customers statewide. Whether it is designing service for a new major employer or maintaining the system around the clock, the people of PNM embody the spirit of personal commitment that customers expect and deserve.

The dedication of PNM to dependable electricity is vital to operations for the area's high technology companies, whose energy needs are some of the most demanding in the world. In fact, the ability of PNM to keep the lights on 99.99 percent of the time has earned it title of the most reliable electric provider in the nation by the Edison Electric Institute. And while such dependability might seem to affect cost, the truth is, PNM commercial electric rates have declined 19.5 percent since 1994 and they are expected to drop another 2.1 percent in September 2005.

As a company that believes environmental stewardship makes good business sense, PNM has positioned itself to be a national leader in renewable electricity. The company offers PNM Blue Sky ™ from one of the world's largest wind farms in eastern New Mexico. ◆

Within the ultra-high tech PNM Power Operations Control Center, engineers monitor electricity demand and control power flow 24/7/365 on 2,282 miles of transmission lines across New Mexico.

Rod Reilly

Charles Ledford

BY THE TIME NEW MEXICO JOINED THE UNION
in 1912 under the state motto: "The Land of Enchantment,"
it was home to three distinct, amiably co-existing cultures.
As a tribute to this multicultural heritage, the state flag displays
the red Zia Indian sun symbol against a background of
bright yellow, the color of the Spanish Monarchy.

AN F-16 FLYOVER FROM THE 150TH FIGHTER WING
of the New Mexico Air National Guard marks the Veteran's
Day opening ceremonies, held each November 11 at the
New Mexico Veterans Memorial Park. Located in uptown
Albuquerque and ten years in the making, the memorial is
scheduled to be finished by 2005.

Charles Ledford — All

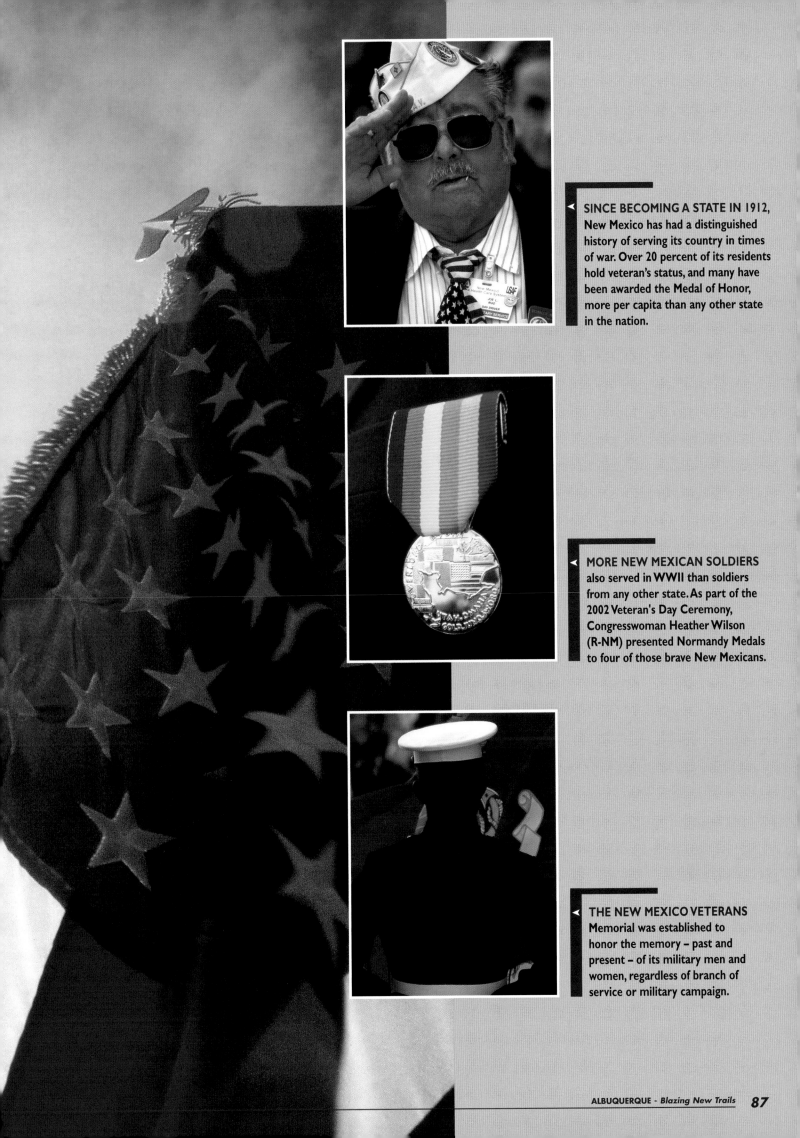

SINCE BECOMING A STATE IN 1912, New Mexico has had a distinguished history of serving its country in times of war. Over 20 percent of its residents hold veteran's status, and many have been awarded the Medal of Honor, more per capita than any other state in the nation.

MORE NEW MEXICAN SOLDIERS also served in WWII than soldiers from any other state. As part of the 2002 Veteran's Day Ceremony, Congresswoman Heather Wilson (R-NM) presented Normandy Medals to four of those brave New Mexicans.

THE NEW MEXICO VETERANS Memorial was established to honor the memory – past and present – of its military men and women, regardless of branch of service or military campaign.

Greater Albuquerque Chamber of Commerce

Nestled between the Sandia Mountains and the Rio Grande Valley, the city of Albuquerque is a powerful economic engine for the state of New Mexico. Balancing centuries of culture with high-tech industry and fast-growing commerce, Albuquerque boasts an evolving economy and an unmatched quality of life.

To represent and enhance the business environment, the Greater Albuquerque Chamber of Commerce has worked for more than eighty-five years fostering a favorable business climate in the Albuquerque metropolitan area. Twenty-six-hundred member firms and more than 150,000 employees make up the Chamber's membership.

The diversity of Chamber members enables the organization to address critical issues in many areas—all with the Chamber's mission of economic development in mind and the attitude that if it's good for business, it's good for the community. Topping the list—education, tax policy, healthcare, water, and economic development.

Education has, for the last several years, been a controversial area of involvement for the state's largest metropolitan chamber of commerce. In the late 1990s, realizing that education was a vital, basic component to economic prosperity, the Chamber took a necessary step in advocating for the reform of Albuquerque's 85,000-student public school system.

The Chamber's education reform initiatives move forward on the premise that every child can learn and be taught. The goals: higher expectations, greater accountability and increased standards, development and support of teachers, literacy, and the involvement of the business community. The effort continues to gain momentum—the primary objective—to ensure a world-class education for all children.

Each year the Chamber supports numerous development, networking, and training events.

Chamber of Commerce board members and membership pause in front of Albuquerque's new Isotopes Baseball Stadium. The Chamber was instrumental in supporting the venue, which brought AAA baseball back to Albuquerque in 2003.

Education is key, but the Chamber's involvement in the community, goes far beyond one issue. Accessible and affordable health care is paramount. The Chamber advocates on behalf of legislation that allows for the development of insurance programs designed with the high number of New Mexico's uninsured in mind.

With a healthy, well-educated community, an abundance of high-quality jobs are necessary. To help meet the demand for jobs in the ever-growing population, the Chamber functions as a necessary piece in business retention and expansion-providing the support and resources businesses needed to grow and evolve.

Efforts also continue toward refining New Mexico's tax policy. The state needs a tax structure that reflects today's changing economy and provides a competitive foundation and the ability to attract high-paying employers to Albuquerque and New Mexico.

Three hundred beautiful, sun-drenched days take their toll on this arid, high desert city, and the Chamber takes issues surrounding the city's valuable water resources seriously—working with many organizations to implement strategies to promote responsible water use, both locally and around the region—ensuring a plentiful supply for years to come.

Bringing members together, lobbying the legislature, promoting responsible growth, just a few ways the Chamber is *covering all bases for business*. The organization's slogan, "Our Business is Your Business" says it all. ◆

IN A WAY, ALL ROADS LEAD TO ALBUQUERQUE.
Economic growth, a temperate climate, and cultural vitality
have kept the city situated at the some of the nation's most
important crossroads, including the Camino Real, Route 66,
and the intersection of two bustling Interstates

Kimo Theate

Route 66 Crossroad

John Nugent

Convention Ctr. / Visitor Info.

g Building

/Sheriff

ourthouse District

Albuquerque Hispano Chamber of Commerce

As an organization dedicated to improving economic opportunity in New Mexico, the Albuquerque Hispano Chamber of Commerce is an influential force in many areas that affect community vitality. With a core mission dedicated to small and disadvantaged businesses, the Albuquerque Hispano Chamber of Commerce (AHCC) opens doors that help new and existing businesses succeed. In addition to housing an office of the Small Business Administration and the Central Area Career Center on its premises, the AHCC works in partnership with businesses throughout the community to facilitate access to a range of amenities. One such partnership has resulted in the development of the new eMercadoNM.com, a virtual business information service linked to the AHCC web site.

The chamber's commitment to economic prosperity is manifest in its new headquarters. Opened in 2001, the AHCC offices are located in the Barelas neighborhood, a once-thriving area of commerce that had seen years of decline. Today, the Barelas community is undergoing revitalization, anchored by chamber-driven activities like the construction of the National Hispanic Cultural Center.

AHCC's offices are also home to the Barelas Job Opportunity Center, a state-of-the-art education and training center offering free, customized classes for members of the chamber and the community. The chamber developed the center following the success of its School to Work initiative, which provides high school students with work-based learning.

For three hundred years the El Camino Real trade route played an important role in Albuquerque's economy. Today, a section of this "royal road" along Fourth Street contains many of the city's businesses and support organizations, including the AHCC, led by President and CEO Loretta Armenta.

ALBUQUERQUE

HISPAN@

CHAMBER OF COMMERCE

Chairman of the Board Jimmy Trujillo (l) and
Chief Operating Officer Phil Castillo meet with
Loretta Armenta to review their strategic plan for
the upcoming year.

Today, the chamber is participating in an
Industry Clusters program that uses partnerships
with businesses to develop industry-specific
training. The chamber educational assistance
also includes providing scholarships for students
at the elementary, middle, and high school levels.

Through its Convention and Tourism arm,
the AHCC fosters economic growth in the state's
largest industry. Whether assisting with the
organization of events, public relations,
competitive bidding for accommodations or
tours, or the distribution of promotional
literature, the chamber's convention and tourism
professionals are helping to generate global
interest in all New Mexico has to offer.

The AHCC also generates interest about Albuquerque business as an advocate at the
legislative level. Each year, the chamber lends its support to legislative activities that promote a
positive business environment and keep Albuquerque competitive in the national arena.

This voice with government is just one of the many reasons for joining the Albuquerque
Hispano Chamber of Commerce. Other benefits of membership include a wealth of networking
opportunities, from monthly Business Exchange El Cambio Luncheons and After Hours
Business Exchanges to the annual La Noche Encantada Annual Gala Banquet. Whatever the
event, AHCC activities consistently attract capacity crowds.

The scope of Albuquerque Hispano Chamber of Commerce activities is astounding
considering that this is a group of just over two dozen personnel and approximately
1,400 members. But it is a group clearly dedicated to enhancing Albuquerque's reputation
for entrepreneurial opportunity. ◆

NEW
MEXICO
LAND OF ENCHANTMENT

OWNER NICK MANOLE'S CAFE occupies quite a historic spot at Central Avenue and Fourth Street. The building once housed Maisel's Indian Trading Post and Brigg's Drugstore and Soda Fountain, both popular stops for Route 66 travelers. Today, locals as well as out-of-towners go for the friendly atmosphere and terrific Greek-American specialties.

NEON SIGNAGE was a popular way to attract travelers along Route 66. As a tribute to Central Avenue's history as part of the nation's Mother Road, many shop owners still retain their shops' original signage, or add new ones in a style that brings one back to another era.

WITH ITS SNAZZY DÉCOR, authentic soda fountain, and jumpin' jukebox, the Route 66 Diner at 1405 Central Avenue NE duplicates perfectly the sights, sounds and tastes of a roadside 1950s diner. Since 1987, people have flocked here for the atmosphere and the food, which includes such retro comfort classics as liver and onions, chicken fried steak, and meatloaf like mother used to make.

Alan Weiner — All

In 1926, Route 66 was a simple strip of two-lane black top, built to connect the 2,448 miles that separated Chicago from Los Angeles. Today, it is a cultural icon.

For forty years, Route 66 carried millions of newly mobile Americans across the country, allowing these travelers unprecedented glimpses into the nature of the expanding west. Route 66 also injected new life into the American tourism industry, which almost overnight developed to accommodate, in increasingly wild and imaginative ways, the needs of road weary travelers. In Albuquerque, where Route 66 passed east to west along what is now called Central Avenue, scores of roadside diners, motor lodges, and souvenir shops sprang up along the length of the route, each one more colorful and neon-lit than the next. Some are still in existence today along Central Avenue, architectural icons of an era long gone, but not yet forgotten.

While most of Route 66 has all but vanished, victim of the superhighway bypasses of the 1970s, Albuquerque remains dedicated to preserving the spirit of America's Mother Road with yearly celebrations, on-going architectural preservation, and an ever-present optimistic spirit that beckons visitors from near and far.

Talbot Financial Corporation

With sixty offices in twenty states and over $2 billion in annual premiums, Talbot Financial Corporation consistently ranks among this country's top twenty insurance brokers. Founded in Albuquerque in 1957 by Lyle Talbot, the company remains headquartered in Albuquerque and is now the largest independent insurance agency in the state.

Under the guidance of current CEO David Weymouth, Talbot continues its tradition of helping clients preserve their property, protect their income, and build financial security. With the resources and capabilities exclusive to a national firm, Talbot is able to focus on the individualized needs of its local clients, offering personal and business insurance programs from over one hundred highly rated providers. Customized employee benefit programs are also available to help companies recruit and retain valued employees.

In addition, Talbot has become one of the country's leading third-party marketers of annuities and mutual funds to financial institutions, banks, and general agencies nationwide. Here again, Talbot offers customized investment programs to fit specific needs as well as training, sales, and marketing support.

Talbot also puts a premium on giving back to the city that helped nurture its success. As well as serving as a Corporate Cornerstone supporter of the United Way of Central New Mexico, Talbot contributes time, energy, and money to dozens of local charitable events and organizations. Every year, Talbot's philanthropic efforts grow, proving that success is all the more sweet when it can be shared. ◆

(l-r) Talbot President and CEO David Weymouth with clients Maryle Barber and Eileen Cook of Casa Esperanza; Talbot Sr. Account Executive Steve Aguilar, and Executive Vice President and Southwest Region President Greg Gates. Talbot professionals are committed to serving the needs of their clients and their community.

Charles Ledford

CASA KIDS CLUB'S WAY TO PLAY
1. Be A Friend. Take Turns And Share.
2. Big Kids Help The Little Kids Have Fun!
3. Play Safe! Enter The Play Area Slowly So You Don't Bump Into Anybody Or Fall On The Gravel.
4. Kids 3-93 Old Can Play. Parents Too.
5. Please Don't Climb On The Wall, On Gates Or On The Outside Of The Playground Equipment.
6. Children Under 5 Years Must Be Accompanied By A Parent Or Other Adult And May Not Be Left Unattended.
7. Rough Play And Foul Language Will Not Be Tolerated.
8. Absolutely No Rock Throwing!

IN A CITY RENOWNED FOR ITS ECLECTIC MIX of architectural styles, FMSM Design Group sets the standard for enhancing quality of life through visionary design. Opened in August 2001, their new Bernalillo County Court House located at Fourth and Lomas is as beautiful as it is functional.

Chuck Young

Alan Weiner

Griffin & Associates

With the average person absorbing nearly three thousand advertising messages a day, it takes creative and unique advertising and marketing campaigns to ensure prospects take notice. That's what sets Griffin & Associates apart from its competitors. The Griffin team produces marketing campaigns that get noticed and produce results.

The firm's mission statement sums up its philosophy: "We at Griffin & Associates are an extraordinary public relations and advertising team that produces outrageous results." Griffin's dynamic, interactive, and synergistic style allows them to stay intimately connected to each other and to their clients. They infuse energy and vitality into their clients' projects and produce the results that make a measurable difference.

"We are our clients' partners in creating strategies that benefit the community and influence the world," says President Joan Griffin. "We like to think we inspire boundless possibilities and turn dreams into reality. We are consistently creative, constantly learning, and we always have fun."

Projects are a collaborative effort between the Griffin and client teams. Thorough research and creative brainstorming sessions set the tone and foundation for each project - whether it be a complete branding campaign, a television commercial, a website, a public awareness campaign or a public relations event. Their eye is always on maximizing the budget utilizing unique creative tools and partnering with other organizations to stretch the budget's effectiveness.

The dynamic team of Griffin and Associates is consistently creative, constantly learning, and always having fun. (Left to right): Ed Waters, Stephanie Bachuzewski, Phyllis Baker, Barbara Rudolf, David Empey, and Joan Griffin (center).

Alan Weiner—Both

"Ditches are deadly, stay away!" is what the Ditch Witch, emissary for the Ditch and Water Safety Task Force, tells students at Albuquerque's Montezuma Elementary School. Each year Griffin and Associates coordinates over one hundred Task Force assemblies and events to teach children about the hazards of playing in and around arroyos and ditches.

Part of Griffin & Associates' success stems from its commitment to community service. Every employee serves on at least one non-profit board of directors, and the company donates hundreds of thousands of dollars annually to non-profits in pro bono services. Some of the organizations that have benefitted from this include the Downtown Action Team, Bosque School, the Barrett Foundation, New Day, the American Heart Association, the Association of Fund-Raising Professionals,

the New Mexico Youth at Risk Foundation, the New Mexico Boys & Girls Clubs, the New Mexico Advertising Federation, the New Mexico Chapter of the American Marketing Association, the National Association of Women Business Owners, the Rio Grande Minority Purchasing Council, and the Greater Albuquerque Chamber of Commerce.

One of the company's long-term goals is to set up a charitable foundation that will provide marketing and advertising services to non-profits at no cost to their organization. Plans are in the works to launch the foundation within the next two years.

The company opened its doors in 1990 with Joan Griffin as the sole employee. Griffin & Associates has grown into a full-service marketing, advertising and public relations firm with offices in Albuquerque, Tucson, and Durango. The company has also added a Web advertising and Hispanic Advertising Division to its repertoire. "Passion and creativity is what we offer," says Griffin. "We are constantly learning and developing additional skills so we can produce the results our clients expect. Staying ahead of the trends and having fun is critical in this business." ◆

MUSEUMS LOCATED THROUGHOUT THE CITY ▶
provide children and adults with the opportunity
to learn about New Mexico's rich and colorful
history. Four Centuries: A History of Albuquerque
is a permanent exhibit at the Albuquerque
Museum featuring installations and collections
illustrating four hundred years of New Mexico's
politics, culture, and society.

▼ **THE WORLD'S LARGEST COLLECTION** of live
rattlesnakes resides at the American International
Rattlesnake Museum in Old Town. Here, visitors
learn about the fascinating habits of several species
of rattlesnakes as well as some of their
non-poisonous brethren.

Rod Reilly — All

THE NAVAJO INDIANS of New Mexico are renowned for their woven rugs. Fine examples of these and other weavings are also on display at the Four Centuries exhibit.

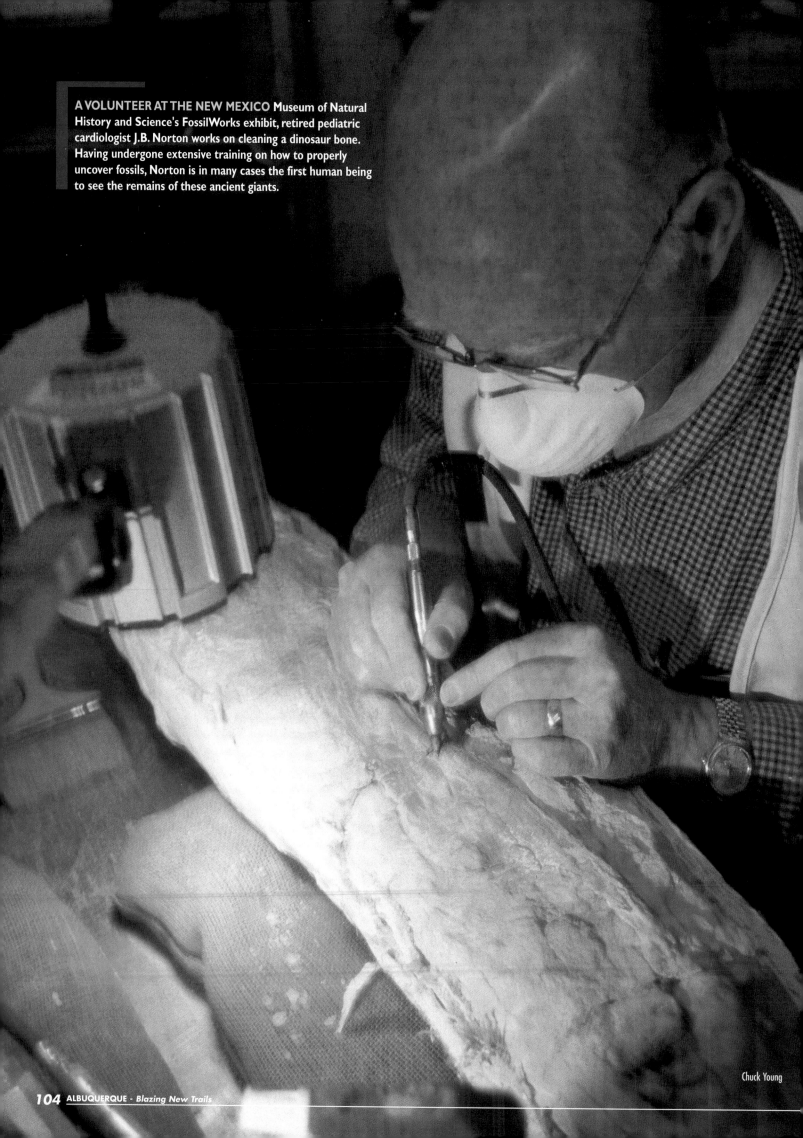

A VOLUNTEER AT THE NEW MEXICO Museum of Natural History and Science's FossilWorks exhibit, retired pediatric cardiologist J.B. Norton works on cleaning a dinosaur bone. Having undergone extensive training on how to properly uncover fossils, Norton is in many cases the first human being to see the remains of these ancient giants.

Chuck Young

KPMG LLP

In business, it is more important than ever to be sure of the bottom line. For KPMG LLP, that "bottom line" represents a commitment to not only serving its clients with the highest standards of professionalism in accounting, auditing, and tax services, but also doing what is right for the community.

With roots dating back more than a century, KPMG has been a part of the Albuquerque landscape since 1956. Since then, KPMG has shown itself to be a substantial contributor to both the economic and social well being of New

Mexicans. In addition to hiring over two hundred University of New Mexico (UNM) graduates over the years, the firm has been a long-time supporter of the university's Presidential Scholarship Program, including the establishment of the KPMG Distinguished Professorship in Accounting at UNM's Anderson Schools of Management.

KPMG personnel know the importance of sharing expertise and supporting their neighbors. From the first day of employment, members of the firm are encouraged to participate in activities involving professional, charitable, and civic organizations. KPMG's personnel have served in leadership positions and provided support to groups like the Greater Albuquerque Chamber of Commerce, United Way, Albuquerque Boys and Girls Clubs, Junior Achievement, and the New Mexico State Board of Public Accountancy.

For KPMG, the factors that make up a successful business are the innumerable ways a professional, caring attitude contributes to the good of the community. ◆

(l-r): Director Tony Strati and partners Cynthia Reinhart, Fred Winter, Jr., Linda Volk, and Anthony Berrett in front of a mural at the New Mexico Museum of Natural History and Science. KPMG is proud to serve as lead sponsor for the museum's annual Chocolate Fantasy fundraiser.

Alan Weiner

ALBUQUERQUEANS HAVE A DEEP AND ABIDING LOVE for baseball, whose rich history in the city goes back to 1880. No wonder the loss of the beloved Albuquerque Dukes in 2000 was such a crushing blow to fans. But when a newly formed team, the Albuquerque Isotopes, took to the field of a completely rebuilt stadium in 2003, it quickly became apparent that AAA baseball would once again reign supreme in the city.

FAN LOYALTY RUNS HIGH and everyone has a favorite player. In turn, each and every team member makes sure to show his appreciation by taking the time to stop and talk to fans.

Rod Reilly — Both

▲ **LT. COL. LEE PERA** gets ready to fly the **CV-22** Simulator to test the **CV-22 Osprey** helicopter's infiltration capabilities as a reconnaissance support aircraft. Kirtland's **58 SOW** wing will be the first at the base to take on the **CV-22** mission in training the aircrews.

▲ **KIRTLAND AIR FORCE BASE** supports ten **C-130** aircraft, along with a highly trained maintenance crew that ensures the safe transport of soldiers and materiel to and from mission sites.

Rod Reilly — All

IT TAKES OVER 14,000 AIR FORCE personnel and 11,000 civilian contract workers to keep Albuquerque's Kirtland Air Force base running smoothly. Here, a member of the MH-53J Pavelow helicopter crew guides the aircraft into its hangar for routine maintenance.

Modrall Sperling

At Modrall Sperling, we focus on delivering the very best service to each of our clients. Any good lawyer can tell you what the law is, but clients need to know how the law affects them. That's why understanding a client's business is our first priority. Without understanding, lawyers can lecture about the law; with it, lawyers can provide effective counsel.

Going above and beyond simply interpreting the law is a tradition for a firm that dates back to 1915, when Judge John F. Simms began a practice based on the highest standards of integrity. Since then, we have continued to draw talent like governors, a state senator, state supreme court justices, district court judges, United States attorneys, the first female president of the American Bar Association, and the first Hispanic female president of the State Bar of New Mexico.

As one of the oldest and largest firms in the state, chances are we already know your industry through past transactions, litigation, advice, or support of industry groups. From there, we listen, knowing that each client, each matter, is an opportunity for us to learn more about people, about industries, and about your business.

Today, more than seventy attorneys practice from offices in Albuquerque, Las Cruces, Santa Fe, and Roswell. Throughout this scope of operations, we emphasize communication to ensure our services meet our clients' needs, whether that means off-hours availability, a case-specific extranet, or other avenues of communication utilizing s tate-of-the-art technology.

Attorney Doug Schneebeck embodies the firm's belief that contributing to the community is an important route to growth as a lawyer. For three years Doug has helped student athletes reach their potential in his position as volunteer hurdles coach for the University of New Mexico track team.

Alan Weiner

Attorneys Walter Stern (r) and Meg Meister confer with Louis Abruzzo, president of the Sandia Peak Tram Company, a client for over nine years. Most recently, Modrall Sperling represented the company in the Pueblo of Sandia land claim.

Our strong internal relationships foster the collegiality and trust that allows us to apply our diverse expertise to provide integrated solutions. For example, our team-based approach allows us to combine tax and Indian law analysis with the basics of a real estate transaction, or to use our knowledge of the oil and gas industry to help defend related personal injury claims.

We use the same ability to build relationships to benefit the community, leading organizations ranging from New Mexico First to the New Mexico Symphony Orchestra. Such leadership strengthens the community and allows us to grow as lawyers by developing our ability to work and communicate with people with diverse backgrounds and interests. Perhaps the most visual representation of our community support can be seen in our in-house art collection, compiled largely through support of local artists over the past forty-five years.

The law is not a static set of rules, but a collection of dynamic principles evolving over time. To make good decisions, clients need dynamic counsel who understand both the direction of the law and the direction of their clients' businesses. Modrall Sperling has provided such counsel for the better part of a century, and continues to provide it to our exceptional clients today. ◆

EACH OCTOBER IN ALBUQUERQUE a spectacular display of color erupts from the Bosque as the cottonwoods lining the river's edge exchange their summer greens for autumn's golden hues.

John Nugent

Grant Thornton LLP

For Grant Thornton, a strong community is one where leaders take an active part in building the foundation. "We try to make sure our personnel are involved in the communities that we live in, working with civic organizations that they believe in," says Kim Nunley, managing partner and assurance partner. Consequently, Grant Thornton's personnel foster an ever-improving quality of life by participating in a number of professional and charitable organizations.

A favorite benefactor of Grant Thornton's giving is Junior Achievement of New Mexico, a non-profit organization that teaches youth about the free enterprise system, the importance of community, and the benefits of staying in schools. In addition to board service and fundraising efforts for the organization, Grant Thornton personnel volunteer to share their expertise with youth in area schools. It is an activity the firm's members freely admit is a two-way street. "We get back every bit that we give—and then some," says Kim Nunley.

Of course, Grant Thornton is committed to providing services that build a strong business community, specifically where the needs of middle market companies are concerned. "Our focus on the middle market suits Albuquerque very well," says Nunley, "especially since the types of businesses here are typically the entrepreneurial, owner-operated companies."

More than 100 years of combined experience at the partner and manager level enables Grant Thornton to serve companies with matters ranging from complex tax laws to technology management to improving operations.

(l-r) Cory Lundy, Lisa Todd, Kim Nunley, and James Chyz. GT helps middle market companies navigate complex tax, assurance, and compliance matters.

GT Accountant Annalee Lister with Junior
Achievement of New Mexico President
Mario Burgos at the Junior Achievement
Bowl-A-Thon. GT's participation in activities
like the Junior Achievement's annual bowling
fundraiser is helping build a strong
community for tomorrow.

"With that level of expertise, we're able to consult with our clients on issues they face," says
Nunley, emphasizing another advantage of working with Grant Thornton is its global resources.
"If clients have any special interests, or a specialized service need, then we have access throughout
our national and international team to bring that expertise to our clients."

But while the name Grant Thornton may have worldwide impact, it also means personal
attention at the local level. The firm's integrated team approach to practice delivers creative
solutions for client needs. "Communication between our people and the client is important in
helping us best serve them," says Nunley, "which also allows us to bring best practices to
the table."

By sharing their talents with neighbors on both the personal and professional level, the
members of Grant Thornton are counting on a thriving future for the people of Albuquerque.

In a community known for its free and independent spirit, one firm measures success by its
ability to support the groundwork for growth. As an assurance, tax, and business advisory firm,
Grant Thornton LLP knows that producing results is far more than just a game of numbers. ◆

JUST A FEW OF THE FRIENDLY FACES that greet visitors to the Indian Pueblo Cultural Center, l-r: sales assistant Heather Koyawena; assistant to IPCC president Ron Solimon, and Miss Indian New Mexico 2003-04 Paulene Shebala; and American Indian Development Associate Dana Melton. Established in 1976 to educate the public about New Mexico's nineteen pueblos and Navajo and Apache tribes, IPCC features a museum, galleries and shops, extensive archives, traditional dance performances, and a restaurant serving Native American cuisine.

Alan Weiner

John F. Nugent Photography

When it comes to photographing people, it takes a certain insight to truly capture the essence of the individual. In Albuquerque, John F. Nugent uses that special talent to create visually compelling moments in time.

First picking up his camera in New York City, Nugent discovered his love for photographing people early in his career. Whether it was shooting models or events, Nugent took every opportunity to build his portfolio. Soon, his work was garnering the attention of decision makers who chose him for such lucrative assignments as the Macy's Thanksgiving Day Parade, Univisions' "El Fieston En Broadway," and the New York City Marathon to name a few.

Since then, Nugent's assignments have carried him from the streets of Manhattan to the sunny beaches of the Caribbean. And while his work has graced international magazines, national promotions, and local events, bringing him both global exposure and top competition honors, Nugent has also found time to share his expertise with others through self-designed seminars and workshops.

During his more than seventeen years behind the lens, Nugent's dedication to his art has earned the praise of prestigious clientele such as Macy's New York, Chase Manhattan Bank, and The Coca-Cola Company, who comment on his professionalism, versatility, reliability, and especially his ability to imaginatively capture excitement and emotion.

A one-man operation with a broad spectrum of expertise, Nugent will shoot, "whatever's on the end of the phone when I pick it up." In this case a quick-build of a Jehovah's Witness Kingdom Hall in Bernalillo.

Chuck Young—Both

When local models like Angeline Jaime (middle) need captivating images for their portfolios, they often turn to Nugent, who has a passion and skill for capturing people, whether candid or posed.

For Nugent, it's more than just a simple click of the shutter. "Consulting with clients in advance to determine specific needs and to understand their interests provides valuable insight," he says. "This is a people business and when people feel comfortable and at ease in front of the camera, they open up and respond—and that's when the magic starts. It's often the difference between just taking a good photograph and creating something that's truly unique."

In 1998, Nugent brought his talents to Albuquerque, acquiring clients as diverse as The Hyatt Regency Tamaya Resort. The New Mexico Workers Compensation Administration, Best Western Hotels, and New Mexico Woman Magazine. His projects today continue to cover the spectrum, ranging from magazine covers to weddings to annual reports. And while completely at home in his four hundred-square-foot studio, Nugent does enjoy working on location, taking advantage of natural outdoor lighting and the beauty of the region. "I cut my teeth on doing images outdoors and I still love doing them," he says. Indeed, many of his images of people and the striking New Mexico landscapes can be found in the pages of this book, for which the publisher hired Nugent as the only local photographer out of dozens to choose from.

Like any successful artist, Nugent has mastered the art of self-promotion, lining his studio walls with his work, and creating an easy-to-navigate web site that contains a fascinating virtual portfolio netting near-perfect results. "If I can get people to my web site, they will do business with me," he says. Such positive response is easy to understand considering that images created by John F. Nugent are more than photographs to be seen, they are moments to be experienced. ◆

Tim Wright

FALL IS THE TIME when farmer's markets throughout the city are filled with the pungent odor and vibrant colors of New Mexico's recent chile harvests. New Mexico leads the United States in chile production with around twenty thousand acres currently under cultivation.

Sutin Thayer & Browne

The last thing you'd probably expect from a law firm with the reputation of Sutin Thayer & Browne is a mission statement borrowed from a 1950's comedian. But if there's one thing that unifies the forty lawyers it's an across-the-board belief in this quote by Milton Berle: "I believe if opportunity doesn't knock, build a door."

That quote says something essential about the firm. Yes, it has a long, distinguished history in New Mexico and, yes, its expertise is broad and thorough. But it's not your grandfather's law firm.

Founded in 1946 by former Chief Justice of the New Mexico Supreme Court Irwin S. Moise, Lewis R. Sutin, a former judge of the New Mexico Court of Appeals, and Franklin Jones, a former commissioner of the New Mexico Taxation and Revenue Department. From the beginning their approach was innovative and aggressive. Hire one of their lawyers and you don't just get legal expertise, you get a lawyer who knows business and what it takes—not only to be competitive, but to excel. The team at Sutin Thayer & Browne is dedicated to maintaining and establishing knowledge in a wide variety of practice areas, including Banking and Financial Services, Personal Injury and Commercial Litigation, Business and Corporate, Indian Law, Family, Government, Bankruptcy and Creditors' Rights, Employee Benefits, Employment, Estate Planning and Probate, Intellectual Property, Insurance Defense, Public Finance, Liquor Licensing and Regulation, Real Estate, Construction, Water Law, and State and Local Tax.

Albuquerque Office Business Group Seated (l-r): Jean C. Moore, Maria Montoya Chavez, Justin A. Horwitz, Elizabeth S. Kentish Standing (l-r): Elizabeth J. Medina, Anne P. Browne, Graham Browne (1935-2003), Cristy J. Carbòn-Gaul, Jay D. Rosenblum, Jeanne Y. Sohn Not shown: Ethan S. Simon, Helen C. Hecht (law clerk)

Chuck Young—Both

The firm believes in serving federal and stategovernment. Our tradition of service includes positions as the UnitedStates Budget Committee staff member, Commissioner of the United States Equal Employment Opportunity Commission, Commissioner of the Federal Communications Commission, Assistant Secretary of Labor, New Mexico AttorneyGeneral, Director of the New Mexico Division of Alcohol and Gaming and Superintendent of the New Mexico Regulation and Licensing Department.

There's no doubt that Sutin Thayer & Browne also takes seriously its role in public and community service. Active in numerous charitable organizations, Sutin's lawyers provide pro-bono legal assistance to individuals and organizations that otherwise could not afford to hire an attorney. Many of them also serve as officers, directors, and board members, and donate time and funds to dozens of local and state organizations. In building and opening the doors that lead to innovations in the legal industry, Sutin Thayer & Browne not only directly benefits its clients, but also the economic, educational, cultural, and social well-being of the state of New Mexico as a whole.

The firm also has a dynamic presence in Santa Fe. Resident in our Santa Fe office are Saul Cohen, Michael G. Sutin, Robert G.Heyman, Robert J. Werner, Mary E. McDonald, Ray H. Shollenbarger, BenjaminW. Allison, Julia L. Peters and Sylvia R. Johnson. ◆

MEGGAN ZSEMLYE AND ARON RALSTON enjoy the music of local band Dogs on Leash, on stage at the Civic Plaza downtown. Public spaces like the Plaza abound throughout the city, both as areas to relax or to enjoy the sights and sounds of a variety of performers.

Tim Wright

THE PLAZA'S INVITING ATMOSPHERE lures the ➤ lunch hour crowd year round, whether to eat, read, relax or, in the case of G. Dean Doctor, refresh the spirit with a little music.

Alan Weiner

REDW Business and Financial Resources LLC

At its half-century mark, REDW Business and Financial Resources is one of the state's largest accounting and consulting firms. It is a date that represents more than experience with numbers, it represents knowing that what counts in business is understanding people.

REDW was started in 1953 by Nathan Glassman and Sanford Rogoff, partners who operated their accounting firm for two decades before it gained momentum alongside a growing Albuquerque. "It really grew more as a result of just fulfilling what we anticipated our clients needed," says Principal Irvin Diamond, who started with the firm in the 1970s. "Every time there was an opportunity for something we just tried to fulfill it and did what we thought was sensible from a business perspective." Principal Mike Walker also came on board at the beginning of the firm's growth period, participating in its measured expansion beyond traditional tax preparation, auditing, and bookkeeping services into areas such as litigation, business valuation, and retirement planning.

With its added staff and capabilities, REDW became the natural choice for clients relying on local knowledge, a factor enhanced by a shared belief that client success is top priority. "One of the primary reasons for the firm's success is a group of like-minded practitioners who share the same core values when it comes to serving clients," says Walker. "That is to provide technically correct and timely service and products at a cost that will lead them to perceive our value. If you do that as a service firm, then you have a better chance of retaining those clients for a long time."

From its expansive headquarters in the bustling Jefferson business corridor, REDW services clients from industries spanning nearly a dozen states.

John Nugent—Both

Principals pictured front row, l-r: Irvin Diamond, Glen Post, Ralph Huybrechts, Carol Cochran, Ron Rivera, Virginia Stanley, Edward Street. Back row, l-r: Steven Cogan, Michael Walker, Jimmy Trujillo .
Missing from picture: Bruce Bleakman.

The introduction of the full gamut of services also fortified the firm's ability to both attract and retain clients. This second growth trend began in the mid-1990s following a merger with another CPA firm, Erickson Allen, P.C., thus forming the firm of Rogoff Erickson Diamond and Walker LLP.

Today, REDW Business and Financial Services LLC is the holding company for subsidiaries REDW Benefits, REDW Asset Management, REDW Stanley Financial Planners, REDW Technologies, REDW Career Placements, and REDW Trust Company. From the service industries to manufacturing and ranching to retail and banking to tribal and government entities, REDW services clients in nearly a dozen states.

Knowing its success is directly related to the community, REDW fosters a culture of involvement at both the professional and civic levels. "Many good business relationships have come from participating in civic and charitable activities," Walker says. "Giving back to the community is extremely important to us," says Principal Ron Rivera. "We all participate in helping to make our community a better place for us all to live and do business," explains Rivera. Whatever it takes to understand clients, REDW will surely count on this tradition to bring success for the foreseeable future. ◆

John Nugent

A YOUNG EXPLORER investigates one of the painted dinosaurs at the Wells Fargo Dinosaur Stompede 2003 display at Civic Plaza. Featuring one hundred five-foot dinosaurs designed by Dennis Liberty and painted by various local artists, the month-long community public art project benefited the New Mexico Museum of Natural History Foundation.

Presbyterian Healthcare Services

Founded in Albuquerque in 1908 as a five-room cottage for tuberculosis patients, Presbyterian has grown into the largest provider of healthcare services in New Mexico today. While the nature of healthcare has changed dramatically since 1908, Presbyterian's founding principles remain the same. As New Mexico's only private, not-for-profit healthcare system, Presbyterian's driving force is its community spirit and dedication to improving health and taking care of people. The organization has grown from humble beginnings to a statewide system of leading healthcare, the state's second largest private employer and so much more. In 2004, Presbyterian was ranked by Modern Healthcare as one of the top ten integrated healthcare systems in the nation.

"We are uniquely positioned and have the commitment to invest in healthcare so that we create a better tomorrow than what exists today," says Jim Hinton, Presbyterian's president and CEO. "We're New Mexico-based and our dedication to individuals, families and communities in this state expresses itself in everything we do."

Presbyterian offers a network of seven hospitals to serve the people of New Mexico. Presbyterian Hospital in downtown Albuquerque is the largest critical care hospital in New Mexico and houses the state's most comprehensive Heart, Women's and Children's programs. Presbyterian Kaseman Hospital in Albuquerque's northeast heights provides general medical, surgical and emergency services and houses the Presbyterian Cancer Treatment Center, the Presbyterian Behavioral Health Center and the Kaseman Arthritis Center. In 2003, for the eighth year in a row, New Mexicans named Presbyterian the most preferred hospital for overall quality and image in an independent study conducted by the National Research Corporation.

Recognized across New Mexico for providing patient-centered primary and specialty care, the 180-member Presbyterian Medical Group's philosophy extends beyond caring for patients only when they are sick, but focuses on maintaining good health. Presbyterian physicians practice proactive health care through care management, visit planning, phone assessments and walk-in

continued on page 130

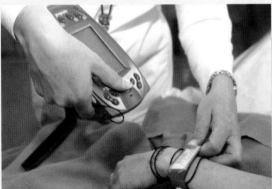

Alan Weiner

Presbyterian's physicians, nurses and caregivers rely on the latest innovations in technology to offer the safest patient care possible. Here, a nurse uses bar code technology to verify the accurate medication for the patient.

Paul Cochran, M.D., and his fellow cardiologists at the Presbyterian Heart Group offer the full range of heart services in the fastest-growing group of heart doctors in New Mexico.

Presbyterian Hospital is New Mexico's largest critical care facility and houses the state's most comprehensive Heart, Women's and Children's programs.

continued from page 129

appointments. Results of this approach include a higher quality of care, disease prevention, more thorough patient visits and increased patient satisfaction.

Presbyterian Health Plan is New Mexico's largest health plan, offering statewide healthcare delivery to more than 1,800 employer groups throughout New Mexico. The Health Plan tailors quality medical management and cost-effective services to meet a wide variety of employer and member needs. It is also the state's largest Medicaid managed care provider and offers a growing Medicare plan, Presbyterian Senior Care.

Eager to compete in a rapidly changing marketplace, Presbyterian's leaders believe they are uniquely positioned for success because they are driven only by what is best for their patients and members. Governed by community volunteers and with a clear goal of becoming national leaders in quality healthcare, patient safety, and stewardship of resources, Presbyterian leverages its not-for-profit model to make investments in the people, equipment and facilities that will continue to improve the health of New Mexicans. Whether it is the recent $80 million at Presbyterian Hospital in advancements for new moms, newborns, children, and heart patients, the new $18 million multi-specialty center in Rio Rancho, or Presbyterian's recognition as one of the "100 Most Wired" hospitals in the nation, the evidence of the organization's commitment to better care runs strong in the city.

While Presbyterian invests $400 million over five years in better healthcare throughout the state, the not-for-profit organization also provides more than $40 million each year in uncompensated care and community benefits. Presbyterian takes pride in its generous community spirit, and provides strong support to the United Way here in Central New Mexico, the Roadrunner Food Bank and the Juvenile Diabetes Foundation.

The Presbyterian Healthcare Foundation also exists as a separate entity to raise and allocate charitable contributions to support present and future needs throughout the Presbyterian system. The Foundation raises and invests significant resources each year to fund programs, and nursing services and other critical healthcare needs in the system. It also directs hundreds of thousands of dollars each year to several health-related community programs throughout New Mexico. ◆

As a hospital system, health plan, and medical group, Presbyterian offers an integrated approach to healthcare with a strong emphasis on wellness and disease prevention.

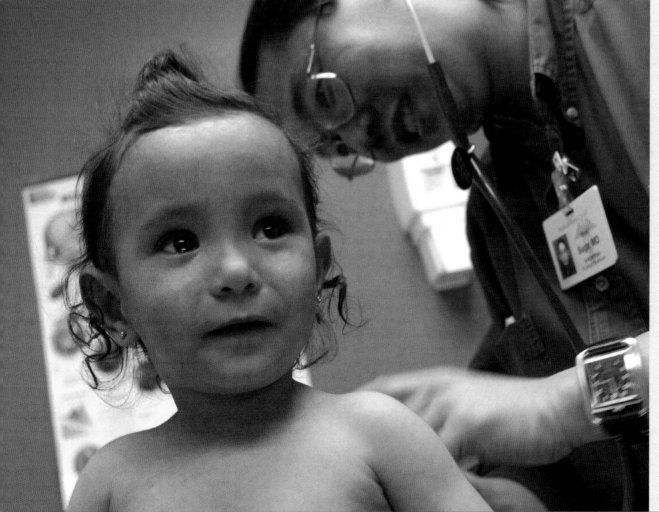

At the heart of Presbyterian is a commitment to the patient, ninety-five years and counting.

LIKE MANY ARTISTS LIVING and working in Albuquerque, abstract landscape painter Frank McCulloch is inspired each and every day by the city's surrounding beauty and plentiful natural light.

Alan Weiner

Cardinal Health/ Allegiance Healthcare

B y providing state-of-the art products and services to hospitals, physicians, manufacturers and research/ development firms, Cardinal Health plays an important role in ensuring quality patient care throughout the world. The Medical Products and Services business of Cardinal Health (formerly Allegiance Healthcare) is specifically involved in the manufacturing and distribution of medical-surgical products. In Albuquerque, the company's Financial Shared Services Center (FSSC) provides credit and collections, accounts payable, and contract administration services. Other Cardinal Health businesses in Albuquerque include one manufacturing site (formerly SP Pharmaceuticals) and two distributions centers— one pharmaceutical and one medical products.

"If you buy from us, work with us, or share with us, you, as a customer, come first," says Kevin Smith, vice president and general manager for FSSC. "We deliver on our commitments, treat others how we would like to be treated, and share goals and rewards."

Founded in 1971 as Cardinal Foods, today Cardinal Health's position as a leading provider of products and services to the healthcare industry has earned them a top ranking in the Fortune 50 companies. Headquartered in Dublin, Ohio, Cardinal employs nearly 50,000 people on five continents, all of them operating under a business philosophy identified by the timeless guiding principles of its founder, Robert D. Walter. These principles include the ethical treatment of employees and customers, constant striving for high performance, innovative thinking, and a collaborative spirit with which they create solutions.

Members of Cardinal's Activity and Communication Team (ACT), who were instrumental in rolling out the new company brand.

John Nugent—Both

GYMNASTICS

Albuquerque's Special Olympics gymnastics team is on their way to the summer games, thanks in part to Cardinal's corporate sponsorship. Cardinal's involvement in New Mexico Special Olympics goes back to 1998 and vice president Kevin Smith (bottom, middle) also serves as the organization's board treasurer.

"I'm amazed at how these principles are woven into everything we do — from employee discussions to internal documents, to annual performance guidelines," says Smith. "Everything's designed around these core values."

Another core value emphasizes community involvement. When FSSC was established in Albuquerque, its first fifty employees were recruited directly from the city's Technical-Vocational Institute (TVI). Many of those employees are still on board, some having worked their way up from entry-level, minimum-wage to highly-compensated, managerial positions. "We're a large company, but we still feel very anchored here in Albuquerque," says Smith.

FSSC is so anchored in fact that the company employs a community-relations representative, Dara Ambriz, who organizes the company's various volunteer efforts. Six years ago, Ambriz organized the Rebel Walkers, a group of FSSC employees who participate in Albuquerque-based run/walks under the motto, "We Walk the Walk." The Rebel Walkers lace up regularly for the March of Dimes, Special Olympics, heart health, breast cancer, diabetes and cystic fibrosis research. This year Ambriz also organized a children's community book drive as part of the Points of Light Foundation's Spirit in Unity of America Project. This project recruits business leaders throughout the country to participate in a community event each year on September 11th.

These projects are only a sampling of the myriad professional and community services provided by FSSC. Although this Cardinal Health business continues to grow and expand its scope, the company's dedication to customer support at a local, national, and global level remains constant and unchanged. ◆

LED BY MUSIC DIRECTOR Guillermo Figueroa, the New Mexico Symphony Orchestra performs the Damnation of Faust, a Dramatic Legend in Four Parts at the Berlioz Festival commemorating the one hundredth anniversary of the composer's death.

SINCE 1932 THE NMSO has entertained audiences with annual seasons featuring classical concerts, pops performances, musicales, and the ever-popular Symphony Under the Stars at the Rio Grande Zoo. Subscriber benefits include ticket price savings, guaranteed best available seating, and ticket exchange and replacement privileges.

UNDER THE DIRECTION OF Roger Melone, the all-volunteer, ninety-one-member New Mexico Symphony Chorus devotes at least two hours per week to rehearsals. Always seeking challenging but appealing works, the chorus was thrilled to honor Berlioz's memory with performances of both Faust and Les Troyens.

Chuck Young — All

Heart Hospital of New Mexico

O n the morning of November 9, 2000, after working a twelve-hour graveyard shift, Albuquerque resident John Bridges found himself in an ambulance having a heart attack so severe his heart stopped several times. Within minutes of arriving at the Heart Hospital of New Mexico's emergency room, Bridges was revived, underwent surgery, and was discharged seven days later. During his stay, Bridges remained in one room from admittance to discharge, his family was allowed to visit twenty-four hours a day, and his room was equipped with sleeper-chair for his wife to stay overnight.

Bridges attributes his recovery in large part to the focused care he received at the Heart Hospital. "I was told I had suffered as bad a heart attack as a person could have. But they were ready for me. They didn't waste anytime getting me from the emergency room to the cath lab. The whole concept is set up to save lives quickly."

Established in 1999 in Albuquerque, the Heart Hospital of New Mexico is a combination of physicians from two leading cardiovascular groups, the New Mexico Heart Institute (NMHI) and the Southwest Cardiology Associates (SWCA). Together, these physicians had as their vision the construction of a facility dedicated entirely to preventing and treating heart disease. In collaboration with MedCath, a North Carolina-based firm that manages cardiac hospitals nationwide, they developed, designed, and now own and operate the Heart Hospital of New Mexico. "We are unique in the medial care industry because most hospitals are not run by physicians and are not single-service oriented," explains Dr. Harvey White. "But being physician-conceived, the physicians retain four board memberships and remain intimately involved in running the hospital."

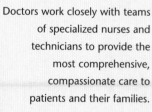

Doctors work closely with teams of specialized nurses and technicians to provide the most comprehensive, compassionate care to patients and their families.

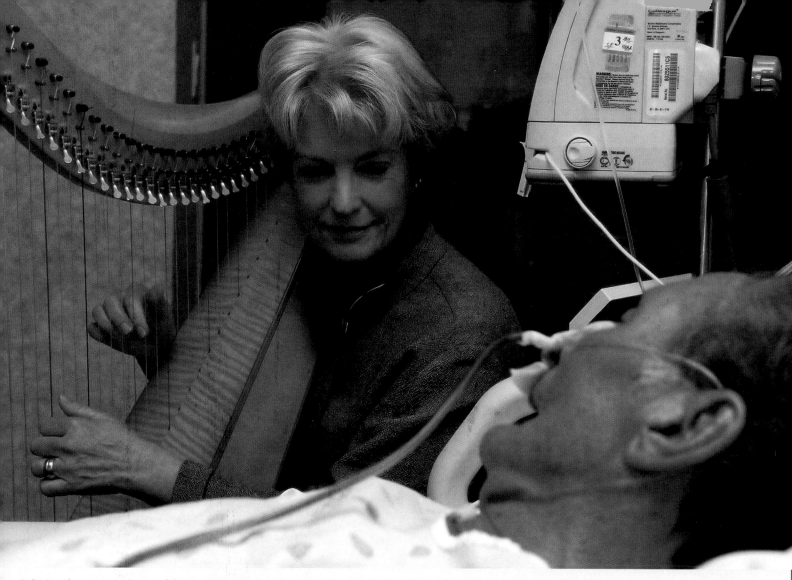

Believing that recovery is one of the most important aspects of treatment, the Heart Hospital provides a number of innovative post-operative treatments, including the soothing sounds of a harpist who visits patients once a week.

From the beginning, it was a team-oriented process, with the focus not just on fighting heart disease, but on changing the way heart care is delivered. When seconds can mean the difference between life and death, the founding physicians knew they had to figure out how to offer the same high quality care in much less time.

One way in which they did that was to locate all important facilities on the first floor (the whole hospital has only two floors). In this way, no time is wasted getting up and down elevators or navigating labyrinthine corridors. In addition, patient rooms are located around four nursing pods, which in turn are located within moments of the cath labs, radiology, and operating rooms.

Says Dr. White: "We have consolidated all our inpatient care into a much smaller facility that enables us to make rounds more efficiently, interact with nurses more easily, and complete and find test results more easily."

continued on page 140

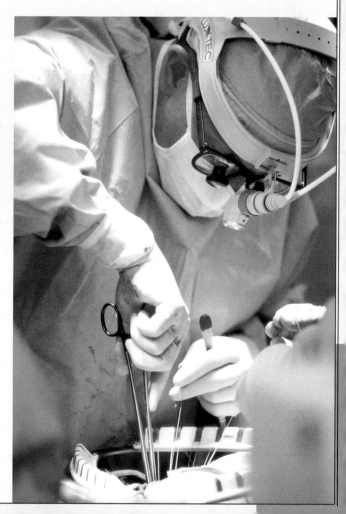

The Heart Hospital's team of surgeons specializes in treating cardiac, vascular and thoracic disease, with open-heart surgery being the most common of their treatment procedures.

Rod Reilly—All

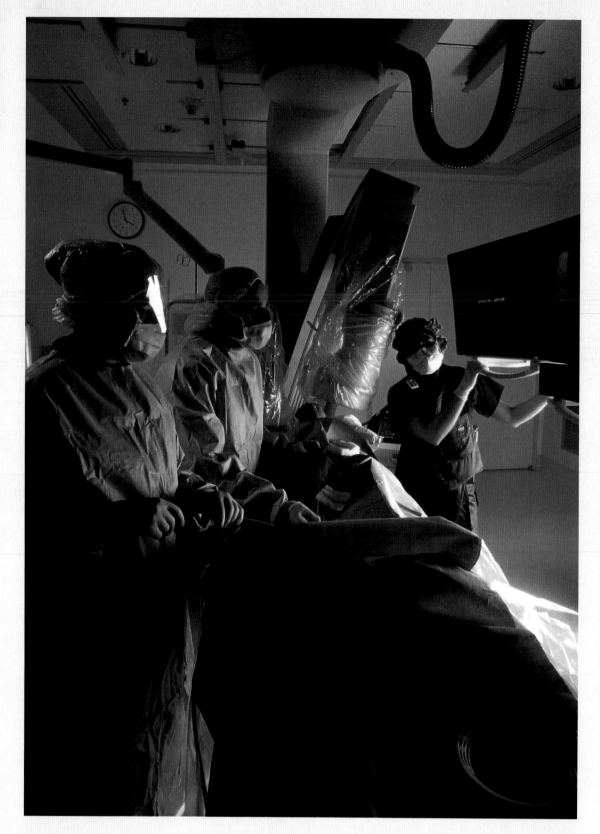

Designed by heart surgeons for heart surgeons, the hospital's three identical operating suites feature high tech airflow systems for optimal infection control, more space to accommodate staff and equipment, and easy accessibility from emergency and patient rooms.

Rod Reilly—All

continued from page 139

The second goal was to minimize stress and maximize recovery by establishing a patient and family centered care environment. From admittance to discharge, each patient remains in one of fifty-five private rooms designed to provide every level of care, further reducing the need to move the patient. Rooms are also equipped with a sleeper chair so that a family member can spend the night. Likewise, there are no restrictions on visiting hours. "I think we learned from the pediatric model that when the family is involved, recovery is quicker," says Dr. Howard Zeman, another founding physician. "Family members have fewer worries or surprises when they get home because they've been through it all at the hospital."

State-of-the-art diagnostic imaging provides quick and convenient testing for inpatients and outpatients.

As a result, Heart Hospital's feedback surveys report patient satisfaction at 98 percent-one of the highest in the industry. Dr. Zeman attributes this to their specialty focus. "We can concentrate on specific pathways or models rather than trying to make the whole hospital efficient."

Efficiency has been further consolidated with the construction just to the south of the hospital of a new 36,500-square-foot office complex. Spread over almost three acres, the facility houses 17 cardiologists, 4 surgeons, and 118 staff members.

To patients like John Bridges, this means that New Mexicans can rest easily knowing they have access to such innovative, concentrated care. "God forbid you ever have to be in a hospital. But if you do, I can't think of a better one to be in." ◆

As dedicated to disease prevention as they are to treatment, the Heart Hospital's 200 physicians, specialists and staff make it their mission to give the Southwest the very best place for healing hearts.

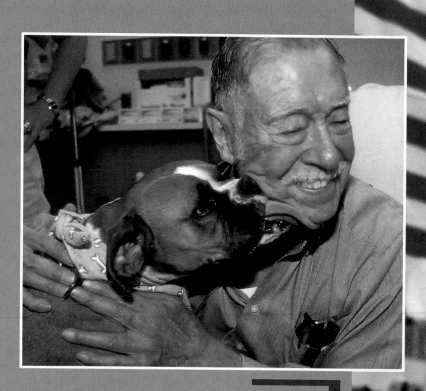

PEOPLE WHO MIGHT BE SHY with strangers often talk to dogs, an act that provides an invaluable outlet for thoughts and feelings. In addition, stroking a dog or cat has proven to reduce blood pressure while providing excellent exercise for hands and arms.

MOST IMPORTANTLY, AN ANIMAL visit provides entertainment and companionship. Patients become more active and responsive during and after visiting with therapy animals.

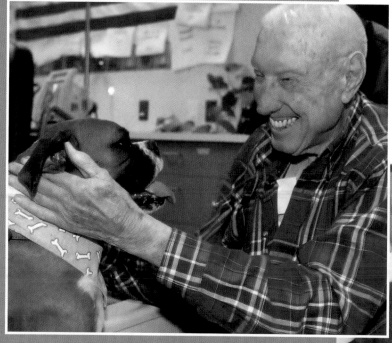

Rod Reilly — All

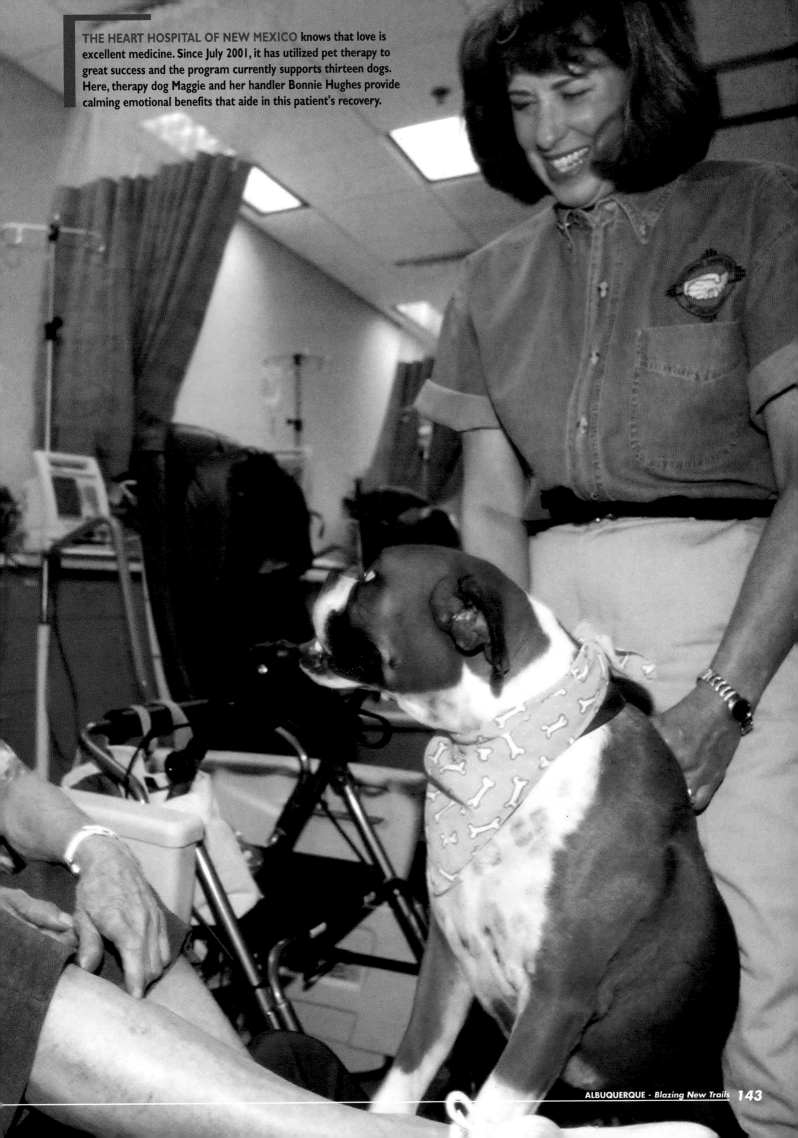

THE HEART HOSPITAL OF NEW MEXICO knows that love is excellent medicine. Since July 2001, it has utilized pet therapy to great success and the program currently supports thirteen dogs. Here, therapy dog Maggie and her handler Bonnie Hughes provide calming emotional benefits that aide in this patient's recovery.

United Blood Services

Each Spring, high school seniors like Emilio Huertaz cross the graduation stage on their way to making a difference in the world. For Emilio's mother, Terry, that walk has even greater significance. "Ten years ago, I couldn't think this far away," she says. "I was so frightened this year would never come. But I'm so grateful that it's here, and my son has been able to go on and live a very healthy life because of all the work involved, including that of United Blood Services."

As the community blood center, United Blood Services provides patients like Emilio with the life-saving blood used in transfusions. Diagnosed with Fanconi's Anemia as a young boy, Emilio was kept alive by transfusions of both blood and platelets in the months before receiving a bone marrow transplant.

Since the opening of its first donation center in Albuquerque in 1951, United Blood Services has grown into a service area of more than forty hospitals throughout New Mexico and the Four Corners region. Today, automated blood collection technology allows United Blood Services to expand and target volunteer blood donations to meet the needs of patients with diseases such as cancer, as well as trauma from auto accidents or severe burns.

David Ray, owner of Moneysworth Automotive, Inc., was a long-time platelet donor, until a hang gliding accident left him in a life-threatening position and requiring multiple blood transfusions. "It was a funny turning of the tables to be on the receiving end," says Ray. "But I felt very grateful to the people who donated the blood, because without it I would have died." When he is able to give blood again, Ray knows the friendly skilled United Blood Services' staff will give him the proper welcome. "Everyone there treats you like a hero," he says.

There's no mistaking the mission behind these red walls. In addition to providing an adequate blood supply and related components to New Mexico and the Four Corners region, United Blood Services also supports research in the fields of blood services and transfusion medicine.

Chuck Young

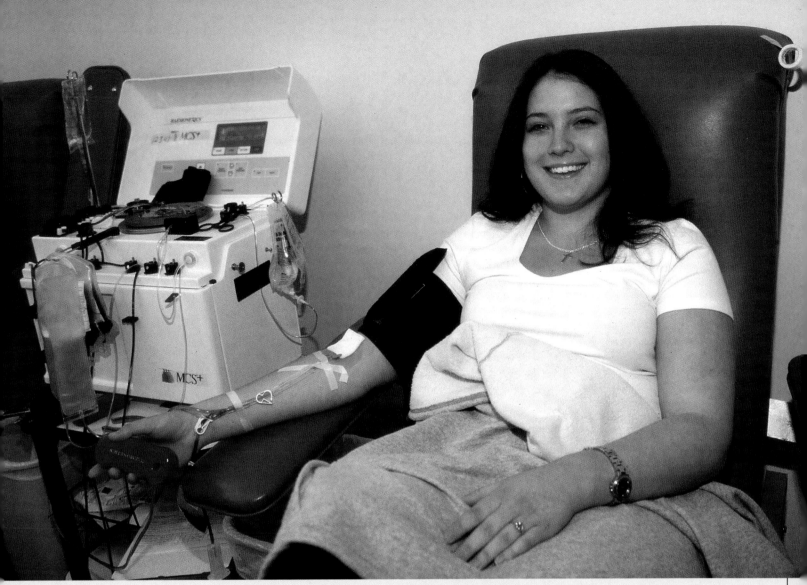

John Nugent

Long-time donor Whitney Waters is among the tens of thousands of "heroes" who give blood to those in need each year.

United Blood Services continues to be a leader in innovative and safe blood collection. The executive director, Morris Dixon stated, "All of us at United Blood Services are committed life-saving professionals. We will strive to continue and expand our level of service for the sake of the patient and the families we serve today and in the years to come." ♦

The United Blood Services staff works diligently with hospitals and doctors to ensure that blood is always available whenever it is needed. Each day, over 250 volunteer "heroes" help keep United Blood Services' shelves stocked with life–saving blood. From students and senior citizens to families and employees, New Mexicans donate year-round at area schools, businesses, government entities and even retail outlets. Local media provides urgent need coverage and donors line up at local collection centers and mobile units to help save the lives of their neighbors.

Lead technician James Salas performs vital quality, inventory, and delivery control functions for the Hospital Services divsion.

John Nugent

LOCALS LIKE FIVE-year-old Storm Taylor and her mother Julie love to stroll through Old Town in the fall, when the days are sunny and mild, the air is filled with the smell of roasting chiles, and the city begins to gear up for the holiday season.

Charles Ledford

Eye Associates of New Mexico, Ltd.

Before Eye Associates began, eye care in New Mexico mostly consisted of general ophthalmology or optometry practices addressing basic concerns, while patients with more complex cases were sent outside the state. Today, all that has changed as thousands turn to Eye Associates of New Mexico for both ordinary and urgent needs.

Eye Associates is the brainchild of the colorful and beloved Albuquerque ophthalmologist Dr. Gerald Rubin. At Dr. Rubin's request, Dr. Robert Reidy and Dr. Steven Cobb joined him in forming the three-doctor practice that opened its doors in 1976. Soon, Dr. Arthur Weinstein, a corneal specialist, joined Eye Associates, spearheading the group's focus on subspecialty care that early on included Dr. Reidy's expertise as the state's first retinal specialist.

From the beginning, the doctors of Eye Associates knew they were creating something special. For example, when the practice co-sponsored free glaucoma screenings in its downtown Albuquerque office, lines stretched around the block, and the staff worked into the night to help check thousands of people for early signs of the vision-threatening disorder. When a specialist went to operate in a distant office, the technical team bundled into the car as well-something that happens less often today because of on-site technical staff. And as those early patients returned for checkups, with family members who needed care, or even just to say hello, the staff became more and more familiar with their needs and their lives.

True to its mission, Eye Associates quickly spread its quality care from beyond its Albuquerque roots into the entire region. Over time, the practice attracted some of the best specialists in the country, nationally recognized physicians who traveled to towns statewide to provide treatment and perform surgery. In addition, the practice added area-wide offices, which now include locations in more than a dozen cities around the state.

(l-r) Dr. Arthur J. Weinstein, Chairman, and Dr. Robert W. Reidy, President, in front of Regina Hall Clinic in Albuquerque.

Chuck Young—All

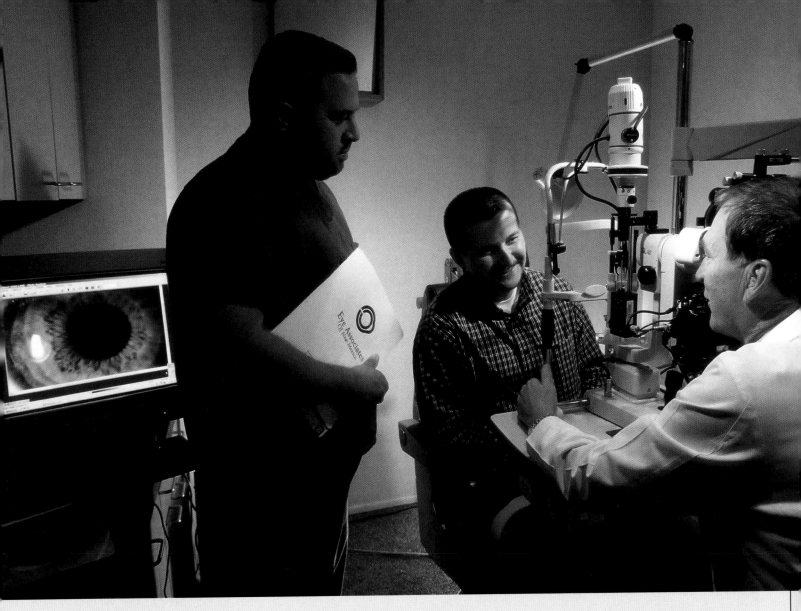

Dr. Michael L. DiMonaco (r) explains the importance of digital-slit lamp technology to ophthalmic technicians, Eric Nieto (l) and Sammy Garcia (middle).

Tucumcari, New Mexico. On a yearly basis, The Eye Associates perform over 159,000 medical procedures and 18,000 surgical procedures. Amid this expertise is a congenial practice environment that fosters a collaborative effort in vision care.

continued on page 150

Today's Eye Associates offers the full gamut of services ranging from general examinations and eyeglass prescriptions, as well as subspecialties ranging from refractive surgery to neuroophthalmology to care for corneal damage and disease. Made up of twenty-eight physicians, twelve clinic locations, and seven optical shops, Eye Associates is based in Albuquerque, with community clinics located in Clovis, Espanola, Farmington, Gallup, Las Vegas, Los Alamos, Santa Fe, Socorro, Rio Rancho, and

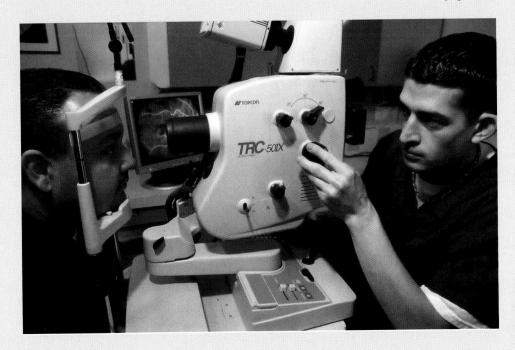

(l-r) Lab Technicians Paul Romero and David Herrera demonstrate a fluorescein angiography a procedure that checks for retinal health. A Fundus digital camera records images of the retina to be printed out or stored in the computer as part of a patient's permanent file.

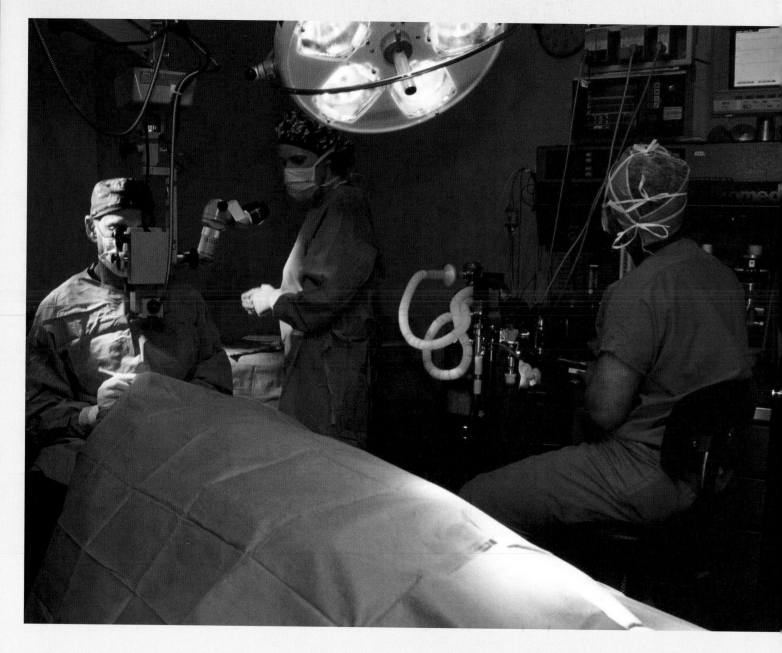

continued from page 149

Specializing brings an enormous quality advantage to our patients," says Dr. Weinstein. "We share our patients, so that they are cared for by the doctor most qualified to treat their problems. This way, we all work on the problems we're best at, and patients see doctors who have much deeper, stronger expertise."

Eye Associates was also the first physician group in New Mexico to establish a stand-alone eye surgery center. Its new Santa Fe center makes it especially easy for patients to receive the full continuum of care by combining eye surgery facilities, examination rooms, and an optical shop in a single location. And in a unique collaboration, Eye Associates has joined with a group of local ophthalmologists and Presbyterian Hospital to create the new Albuquerque Ambulatory Eye Surgery Center, for patients in the state's core.

Without question, the remarkable success of Eye Associates can be directly attributed to the support of patients who have placed their trust in the group. It is a confidence resulting from the delivery of the best possible eye care. "When you give people the most qualified doctors, they have good outcomes, and that's what our practice is built on," says Dr. Weinstein. Dr. Reidy concurs: "We are here to give the absolute highest quality of care. Each and every person in the organization knows that's our mission. It's always been our mission, and we all work to support it."

The Ambulatory Eye Surgery Center in Albuquerque offers a full range of outpatient services including state-of-the-art "no-stitch" cataract surgery, demonstrated here by Dr. Arthur Weinstein and his assistant Anne Dwyer.

Although Eye Associates is now considerably larger than the "small family" that started the practice in the late 1970s, its unified focus remains on the best care of the individual. It is care that extends into the community through participation in activities that continue to include free screenings as well as working with the Lions Eye Bank. "We are dedicated to our patients and our community, and that's never going to change," Reidy promises. "We know that we've been successful for more than twenty-five years because our patients trust us, and we work hard to make sure we deserve that trust. We're here to give the best eye care to the citizens of New Mexico and the Southwest." ◆

Opened in October 2002, the Santa Fe clinic provides full-service eye care to patients throughout Northern New Mexico and Southern Colorado.

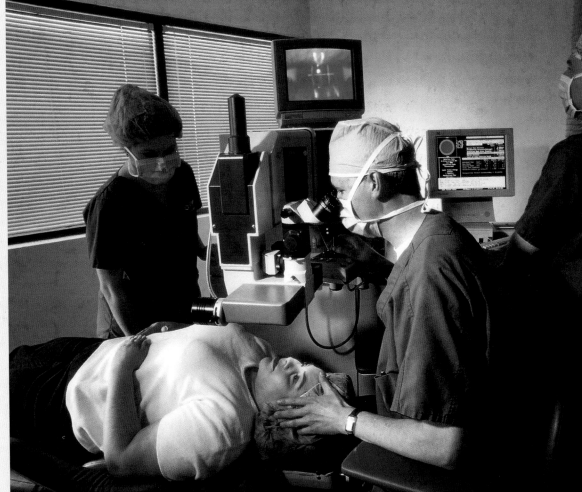

Assisted by Marisa Ragsdale (l) and Danny Perea (r) Dr. Mark P. Lesher performs LASIK surgery at the Albuquerque facility. Along with Dr. Arthur Weinstein, Lesher is recognized by Laser Vision Centers, Inc. as being among the top one hundred LASIK surgeons in the United States.

Chuck Young—All

JAN AND STAN ROTHELL OF LOS LUNAS, NM, put the final polish on their 1940 Mercury Convertible, an entry in Albuquerque's Annual Old Route 66 Car Show. Between 200 and 300 cars are entered each year in July to commemorate the Mother Road, traveling from the National Hispanic Cultural Center to the only spot where Route 66 crosses itself (Central and Fourth Street), and on into Bernalillo at the northern edge of town.

John Nugent

Blue Cross and Blue Shield of New Mexico

Amid the ever-changing challenges of delivering quality health insurance products, Blue Cross and Blue Shield of New Mexico* provides a sense of stability for its members. Since its founding in 1940, Blue Cross and Blue Shield of New Mexico (BCBSNM) has grown into a leading health plan resource. It is a growth based on the ability to anticipate, and respond to, the changing needs of the state's insured.

Today, BCBSNM meets the needs of New Mexicans with a full continuum of benefit plans. In addition to group benefits through Point-of-Service, PPO, HMO, and consumer model health plans, Blue Cross and Blue Shield of New Mexico offers individual coverage, as well as Medicare Supplemental, dental, life, and disability plans.

The acquisition of BCBSNM by Health Care Service Corporation, which also operates the Blue Cross and Blue Shield Plans of Texas and Illinois, has strengthened its financial security and enhanced access to technology resources.

But the real core of the high-quality services provided by BCBSNM is its dedicated personnel. From round-the-clock customer service to ongoing initiatives for improving customer satisfaction, BCBSNM employees understand why their activities are so vital to the company's success.

That sense of contribution is instilled by the senior management team, which is quick to recognize devoted employees. It is the people who answer phones, work with employers, and keep the health of New Mexicans at the forefront of the company's concerns at all times who have guided BCBSNM to its current level of achievement.

By innovatively adapting to the changing needs of the community, BCBSNM continues to grow in scope and services. The company's north campus on Alexander Boulevard, opened in 2002, provides space to nearly double in size.

Tim Wright—Both

The landmark BCBSNM building on Indian School Road NE symbolizes the stability and strength of one of the state's largest employers. For more than sixty years, BCBSNM has provided New Mexicans with a reliable source of quality health care plans.

The commitment of the BCBSNM staff also comes from a long-standing tradition of focusing on four core values: integrity, responsibility, mutual respect, and corporate citizenship. Integrity guides the BCBSNM business practices, providing a tenet for dealings that are honest and forthright. Responsibility gives the company a sense of accountability for its actions. Mutual respect creates an open and responsive working environment. And corporate citizenship is a cornerstone of the company's organization.

More than eight-hundred employees uphold the company's commitment to corporate citizenship, making both an economic and social impact on communities around the state. The company actively sponsors initiatives that enhance community life in areas such as economic growth and improved health for all members of society. The Blue ACE (Active Community Enrichment) team, comprised of employees and their families, gives countless volunteer hours in support of projects that feed the homeless, enrich the holidays, aid during disasters, and help people with health issues and chronic disease.

For New Mexicans who want quality health insurance, Blue Cross and Blue Shield of New Mexico offers a reliable resource for all their needs. ◆

*A Division of Health Care Service Corporation, a Mutual Legal Reserve Company,
an Independent Licensee of the Blue Cross and Blue Shield Association.*

WHO SAYS COWS CAN'T FLY? For two weeks each year, Airabelle the Creamland Dairy Cow takes to the air, accompanied by an assortment of other normally land-locked objects in the balloon Fiesta's special shapes ascensions.

Tim Wright

Albuquerque International Balloon Fiesta®

Like a giant fireworks display, the Albuquerque International Balloon Fiesta fills the skies over New Mexico each year with a mesmerizing spectacle of color. But this is more than an exciting air show, it is a vibrant expression of New Mexican spirit.

From a gathering of thirteen air craft in 1972, the Balloon Fiesta has grown into the world's largest balloon event, drawing hundreds of entries each year. Today, guests and volunteers are an integral part of the action, each staying true to the Balloonmeister's credo that having fun is the criteria for winning.

Host to world championship and cup races over the years, the Balloon Fiesta has earned a reputation for competition that ranges from amusing to truly amazing. Competitions that test maneuvering skills have run the gamut, from target races dropping shrubs and ping pong balls, to grabbing a set of keys from a thirty-foot pole, no challenge is too great for pilots from around the world.

Balloon Fiesta enchantment continues well into the evening, with thrilling sights like the Balloon Glow® and Night Magic™ Glow, where hundreds of tethered balloons light the nighttime hours. Animals, shoes, and vehicles rise into the sky in the Special Shape Rodeo™. Ground activities include parties, shopping, musical entertainment, and more.

With so much wonder and excitement to behold, it is no wonder hundreds of thousands are drawn to this annual manifestation of community spirit. ◆

Mass ascensions are eye-opening experiences for guests of the annual Balloon Fiesta. These glorious morning spectacles provide the perfect start for a day of fun, competition, and games.

Cindy Petrehn

▲ **THERE ARE PLENTY OF LIGHTS, CAMERA, AND ACTION OFFSTAGE** as well, as the performers commemorate the friendships that exist between members of this close-knit troupe. Founded by Suzanne M. Johnston in 1972, the New Mexico Ballet has since become a vital member of New Mexico's performing arts community.

Nugent — Both

ATTENDING A PERFORMANCE OF TCHAIKOVSKY'S NUTCRACKER BALLET has become a holiday tradition for many Albuquerque families. Performed each year for three days at the end of November, the Nutcracker is a co-production of the New Mexico Ballet Company and the New Mexico Symphony Orchestra.

Ever-Ready Oil Company

One of the largest companies of its kind in New Mexico, Ever-Ready Oil Company has a reputation for personalized service that goes back to 1929. That's when Nugget Grossetete, Sr. started the company with his brother and parents in a small garage off Harvard and Central Avenue. Every day, Nugget would drive to Artesia, New Mexico, to pick up the 1,000 gallons of gasoline needed for the family's business. At the end of the day he went door-to-door in Albuquerque to sell his remaining fuel.

That kind of hands-on involvement set a precedent for future growth and success. By 1984, Ever-Ready had become the primary distributor for Chevron in New Mexico and in 1986 it built its first Redi-Mart convenience store and gas station in Albuquerque. In the mid 1990s, Colorado native Charles Ochs moved to New Mexico and purchased Roger Cox Petroleum and Patterson Oil. Envisioning the potential for increased profitability and employee opportunity, Ochs purchased Ever-Ready Oil in 1998 and merged the three companies into one.

Today Ever-Ready is one of the state's largest fuel distribution companies, with an impeccable safety record, a retail business that includes thirty Redi-Marts statewide, and a wholesale business that provides fuel, lubes, chemical, and specialty products to industrial and commercial customers throughout the southwest. But despite its growth, the emphasis on personal service remains. For instance, the Redi-Marts, provide a large array of on-the-go products ranging from gasoline and automotive products to food and beverages. Likewise, the wholesale division offers a convenient card lock system in which, with one swipe of a card, major customers can obtain any amount of fuel at any time of day with customer security options.

Travelers throughout New Mexico can count on the familiar red, white, and blue Chevron Redi-Marts for competitive prices, high quality, and a multitude of items for those on the go.

Chuck Young

By operating and maintaining its own fleet of
trucks and oil tankers, Ever-Ready offers superior
delivery services to all customers.

Ochs attributes Ever-Ready's success to a
core system of values and beliefs based on honest
and respectful dealings with customers and
employees alike. The company motto, "Excelling
in a Changing World," reflects Ever-Ready's
dedication to developing a highly trained work
force that maintains a strong commitment to
excellence and the ability to adapt to changing
customer environments and needs.

In return, Ever-Ready employees are rewarded with competitive wages and a generous
benefits plan that includes medical and dental insurance, educational assistance, paid holidays and
vacations, sick leave, group term life insurance, and employee discounts. Ever-Ready is unique
to the industry in that it has its own employee training facility, and promotions to staff and
management occur primarily from within the company.

This partnership between employee and customers, combined with the flexibility and
knowledge to adapt to change, serves as a guide not only for Ever-Ready's day-to-day operations,
but also as the basis for growth and productivity well into the future. ◆

NO DOUBT FIESTA participants can be as colorful as their balloons. In David Fulmer's case, it's almost a necessity, since he's responsible for directing the early morning inflation and ascension of over eight hundred colorful orbs.

Tim Wrig

Victoria's Secret Direct

When Victoria's Secret opened a call center to assist its Ohio locations with catalogue sales, the intimate apparel giant chose the small city of Rio Rancho, located at Albuquerque's northwestern edge. And it wasn't just for the weather. Not only is the area blessed with a diverse, educated workforce, most of that workforce is also bilingual. Since one of the call center's goals was to provide greater service to its Spanish-speaking clients, the city was a perfect match. In addition, Victoria's Secret catalogue orders are taken twenty-four hours a day, seven days a week. Establishing a call center in a later time zone would mean greater efficiency in organizing fashion consultants' shifts.

Five years later, Victoria's Secret Direct has become an integral part of the community. As one of Limited Brands businesses since 1982, the center embodies the philosophy of Limited founder Leslie H. Wexner to provide high-quality goods and services while at the same time giving back to the community through philanthropic efforts.

Limited Brands and Victoria's Secret efforts focus on women, children, and education says Director of Sales Bev McMillan. "As soon as we arrived, we took it upon ourselves to get involved immediately within the community on these issues."

That involvement led to a partnership with the Albuquerque Journal daily newspaper to address domestic violence issues, beginning with annual forums. The center was also instrumental in supporting the funding of Haven House, a shelter for victims of domestic violence located in Rio Rancho. Limited Brands and Victoria's Secret are also major supporters of United Way of Central New Mexico, believing strongly in the community value of its efforts. These efforts, says McMillan, "Make us all proud of our history in Albuquerque." ◆

The Victoria's Secret call center is a perfect example of employer need matching employee ability. In seeking to expand its service to Spanish-speaking customers at home and abroad, the company tapped into Albuquerque's large bilingual community and in the process created six hundred new jobs.

Alan Weiner

IT TAKES ANYWHERE FROM TWENTY TO THIRTY PEOPLE
to inflate and crew a special shapes balloon, like this one flown
by Wells Fargo Bank. Shaped like the company's stage coach
logo, once inflated the balloon holds 160,000 cubic feet of hot air
and weighs 850 pounds.

WELLS FARGO BANK IS ALSO ONE OF THE SPONSORS of the Special Shapes Glowdeos. Held several times during the Fiesta, these colorful nighttime events are a perennial favorite with attendees. Out of over eight hundred plus balloons that participated in one recent Fiesta, about two hundred were special shapes.

Tim Wright — Both

Alan Weiner

IN A LAND WHERE THE SUN SHINES over three hundred days a year, a cowboy hat is more than a fashion statement; it's a necessity. To look good while staying protected, customers come to The Man's Hat Shop at 511 Central Avenue NW, where owner Stuart Dunlap stocks a large selection of some of the finest hats available, like this classic style favored by Farmington resident Peter Jamieson.

Private Balloon Flights

One of the best ways to capture the beauty of the Rio Grande River Valley is from the basket of a Private Balloon Flights Company flight. Seven days a week, from sunrise to sunset, Private Balloon carries riders wherever the wind takes them.

In addition to the guaranteed longest balloon ride around, there are many extras that make a Private Balloon adventure memorable. From the standard flight to a special ride for sweethearts, each package includes champagne, toast with juice, brunch, delightful souvenirs, and the balloonist's prayer upon landing. Weather permitting, riders may also be treated to an exhilarating "splash and dash." And chase crews welcome riders back to earth with transportation to the site of origination. Private Balloon also offers corporate promotions and group discounts for company picnics, birthday parties, family reunions, or any special gathering.

With a fleet of more than a dozen balloons, Private Balloon Flights is the largest operator in the state. New Mexico State Hot Air Balloon Champion Bentley Streett has owned and operated the company since 1995, turning around an existing operation with a new name, new equipment, and new attitude toward customer service. Today his operation employs as many as forty staff and licensed pilots, all devoted to showing riders how to have fun, to be lighter than air, and to chase the dream of flight. ◆

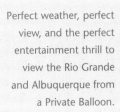

Perfect weather, perfect view, and the perfect entertainment thrill to view the Rio Grande and Albuquerque from a Private Balloon.

Chuck Young

Charles Ledford

BUILDERS IN THE AREA MAKE IT THEIR GOAL to design homes in harmony with the natural environment. Many, like this low profile, pueblo-style building, feature earthen colors and lots of windows to capture solar warmth and the views.

Rod Reilly

NEIGHBORHOODS SITUATED AT THE FOOTHILLS of the Sandias are popular with those who desire expansive views of the city and close proximity to nature and hiking trails. Here, residents have access to numerous mountain trails, plus the ten-mile, multi-use trail that runs parallel to Tramway Boulevard, the city's easternmost north/south artery.

Charter Building and Development Corporation

For many people, the most comforting experience in buying a home is finding a builder they can trust. That is why so many turn to Charter, a company that understands a home is more than a structure, it is a dream come true.

In more than three decades of building homes in and around Albuquerque, Charter has also built a reputation for quality. "We want to build a home, not a house, and there's a big difference in my view," says President Bill Hooten. "We want the home building experience to be something people love, not something they wish they had never done."

For many years, Hooten simultaneously grew one of the nation's largest real estate firms. This experience has helped him recognize the need to build homes that retain their value. In the real estate business, Hooten also gained the insight to meet demand. "From the resale department you knew what the buyers were looking for, so I've always relied on that market and I've always tried to build in the void," he says.

Listening to the changing needs of homeowners led Charter to become a partner in the Building America Program, which promotes the design of homes that are healthier, more comfortable, and more energy efficient. The improved air standards of these homes is just one reason the program has received the stamp of approval from the American Lung Association of New Mexico. "Charter has always been known for its quality and this is just another step," says Hooten. "These homes are designed for mold prevention, affordability, and with all the newest technology."

This elegant, two-story, 3,134 square foot home is Charter's most popular floor plan. With five large bedrooms, three full baths, and a three-car garage, it is versatile and perfect for just about any family.

Charter designs up-to-date floor plans with furniture placement in mind. The Building America Program features also provide homeowners with year-round comfort while helping to conserve on energy bills.

Features of Building America homes that result in near perfect efficiency numbers include foam insulation, low-emittance coated windows, integral wiring, and enclosed ductwork that is tested twice for leakages. Meanwhile, refrigeration and filtered air units keep rooms fresh and to within three degrees difference throughout the house. Satisfied Charter clients are already praising the benefits of these new homes, remarking on their comfort, exceptionally low energy bills, and uniqueness within each community. These features contribute to making Charter's homes Energy Star Compliant.

These days, Charter works exclusively within the Albuquerque metroplex, building neighborhoods like Oxbow North, The Enclave at Oxbow and Seville. Charter also includes special touches like wall niches, ceramic tile entries, laminate stain-resistant kitchen countertops, and more.

To build homes that reflect individual lifestyles, Charter works closely with clients throughout every stage of the home building process, from design and purchase through building inspection. "We have a six page walk through that everyone goes through prior to moving in," says Hooten, "and our objective is to have nothing on that checklist." Charter also offers a superior warranty that extends beyond project completion, and Charter has just been given the 'Elite Builder' designation from the 2/10 Homebuyers Warranty Program.

continued on page 172

continued from page 171

Over the years, Charter Building and Hooten have been known for not only building communities, but in contributing time and resources to organizations that benefit people in need. "I think the fact that the community's been so good to us that we need to give something back to the ommunity," says Hooten, expressing a wisdom that comes from finding great success by making the home buying experience a dream come true. ◆

Beautiful, well-planned
communities are the hallmark
of the Charter name.
The company's considerable repeat
business comes from building
homes with the newest technology
while delivering old-fashioned service.

Charter's well-designed
kitchens are efficient,
convenient, and come
complete with quality
Whirlpool appliances.
Charter also offers many
added options that can
personalize your kitchen
such as HiMacs
countertops and tile
or laminate flooring.

AN ALBUQUERQUE RESIDENT since 1950, abstract multimedia artist Robert Hooten is an active member of the local arts community. Among his many accomplishments, he was a founding member of the New Mexico Arts and Crafts Fair and is a member/contributor to Magnifico Arts, Incorporated, an organization that works to promote the arts through innovative educational programs and exhibits.

Tim Wright

STANDING AS TESTAMENTS TO THE CITY'S deeply rooted faith and reverence for the past, many of Albuquerque's historic Catholic churches, like San Felipe de Neri in Old Town, are not only beautifully preserved, but remain very much in use.

Chuck Young

Enterprise Builders Corporation

EB Enterprise Builders CORPORATION

General Contractor License • #29031

I t was 1988, David Doyle and Ralph Baldwin had just quit their local contracting jobs; each of them had two kids, a mortgage, and bills. Both of them refinanced their homes and each put up twenty thousand dollars. They turned Doyle's laundry room into an office and his garage into a shop.

Today, Enterprise Builders is one of the largest small businesses in Albuquerque. Ninety percent of their twenty million dollars a year in revenue comes from repeat business, the two-man operation now employs fifty, and simple remodels have evolved into over two thousand construction projects that include commercial and retail offices, medical facilities, sports arenas, and athletic gyms for clients throughout New Mexico.

As businessmen, Doyle and Baldwin have kept as their guiding mission the concept of fair play, working to ensure that every step of a construction project, from conception to completion, is a win-win situation for all involved.

That begins with understanding and interpreting their clients' needs and desires, providing them with intense quality assurance and hands-on involvement, and coordinating and communicating with architects, subcontractors, and suppliers to deliver a quality project on time and on budget.

Of course, that kind of exceptional service wouldn't be possible without dedicated employees and Enterprise Builders is equally committed to the success and well being of their staff. The result is low turnover and high loyalty - producting superb construction work for their clients. ◆

David Doyle (President) and Ralph Baldwin (CEO) in front of one of their Award-winning design-build projects, Charter Bank. From small tenant improvements to multi-million dollar design-build facilities, Enterprise Builders Corporation is committed to exceeding their clients' expectations from concept through completion.

Sponsor Supplied

John Nugent—Both

THE ORGANIZATION IS always in need of enthusiastic and knowledgeable volunteers in both fundraising and construction. Some volunteers, like these from Albuquerque's Presbyterian Churches, work at both, going into the community to raise funds and then working side-by-side with recipient families to assist in building their homes.

A LOCALLY RUN AFFILIATE OF HABITAT for Humanity International, the Greater Albuquerque Habitat for Humanity builds over a dozen homes for qualifying buyers each year. Its goal is to provide low-income but financially stable families with well built and affordable housing, like this one in the Puño de Tierra subdivision on Albuquerque's west side

Molzen-Corbin & Associates

For more than four decades, the Albuquerque-based engineering and architecture firm of Molzen-Corbin & Associates has been the company of choice to design and improve the infrastructure of municipalities throughout New Mexico. Molzen-Corbin shapes communities by designing everything from highways, water treatment facilities and airport runways, to city halls, senior citizen's centers, and parks.

"We take applied science and use it to improve peoples' lives," says Adelmo "Del" Archuleta, chief executive officer since 1984. "That means that we produce seemingly ordinary things that you may take for granted in your daily life, for instance the shower you take; the water you drink; or the road, on which you drive to work."

Founded in 1960, the company cemented its national reputation as a cutting-edge engineering firm in the 1970s when the firm's pioneering designs in water resources earned prestigious awards at national and state levels. Today, the firm continues to have a dynamic effect in ensuring safe drinking water for the state's citizens and in ensuring that treated wastewater returned to New Mexico's precious rivers and streams is of the highest purity.

Molzen-Corbin & Associates also keeps New Mexican's lives running safely and smoothly by planning and designing many of the high profile highways, roads, streets, and airport runways that make up the state's transportation network. In addition, the company's team of client-responsive architects designs efficient, safe, and attractive municipal buildings, libraries, parks, and recreational facilities that serve to define a community's unique spirit and culture.

As President and CEO of Molzen-Corbin & Associates since 1984, Del Archuleta has led the firm to national recognition as a premier provider of professional engineering and architectural services, and has been instrumental in assuring a better quality of life for New Mexicans throughout the state.

Rod Reilly—Both

Molzen-Corbin & Associates is known for producing award-winning facilities, such as the above pictured Cogeneration Facility for the City of Albuquerque's Southside Water Reclamation Plant. The consistent excellence of our engineering and architectural design remains unmatched in New Mexico.

Although the firm has won numerous awards for both its engineering and architectural work, Archuleta believes client satisfaction to be the ultimate bottom line. "My goal is to put Molzen-Corbin at the top of the list that says what we did yesterday will make a positive difference to our client tomorrow. What matters most to us when we're done with a job is that our client can shake our hand and tell us that they're proud of us."

The firm's commitment to its valued clients extends far beyond just producing a set of project plans—it's a corporate culture that truly "gives back." Archuleta and his employees have donated tirelessly to numerous professional as well as economic and charitable endeavors in which their clients are involved. For example, Archuleta served as Chairman of the Albuquerque Chamber of Commerce and played a key leadership role in advancing education in New Mexico during his chairmanship. His strong commitment to education led to his appointment in 2003, by Governor Bill Richardson, to the State Board of Education, where he was elected to serve as President of the fifteen-member Board.

Ultimately, through relentless energy, dedication and uncompromised quality, Molzen-Corbin is in the business of improving the way New Mexico lives. "We feel extremely blessed to have that opportunity," says Archuleta. "To know that what we do every day makes a difference in the lives of all of us." ◆

A BEAUTIFUL CAMPUS, DIVERSE STUDENT BODY, and nationally recognized programs attract students from across the globe to the University of New Mexico. Consistently ranking among the best in the nation are UNM's programs in medicine, rural medicine, law, engineering, anthropology, and Latin American and western history.

Charles Ledford

Ray's Flooring Specialists, Inc.

S ince 1970, the owners of Ray's Flooring Specialists, Inc. have made family values their business values. Founder Ray Lucero, Sr. began his career in 1959 as a high school student working summers helping his uncle install various kinds of flooring. "I fell in love with the trade," he says. "There's nothing more rewarding than seeing a customer satisfied by something you've done for them."Eleven years later, Lucero struck out on his own. His garage became a showroom, his dining room an office, and as he went out into the field, his wife Dorothy served as bookkeeper and their children answered phones and relayed messages.

"That's pretty much how we became a family business," says Ray Lucero, Jr., vice president of retail operations. "It's one of our biggest strengths." Brothers Martin, Gerald, Chris and sister Bernadette Frederick also split operational duties.

Today, Ray's Flooring has expanded into two Albuquerque locations-a 16,000-square-foot showroom/warehouse at 2241 Phoenix NE and a 3,200-square-foot showroom at the New Mexico Design Center on Alameda and Jefferson. But although locations have changed, the emphasis on quality customer care and product has not.

Ray's prides itself on a tradition of building familia-like relationships with its customers, some of whom, like Jayne's Corporation, one of the largest construction companies in New Mexico, have been working with Ray's for over thirty years. The company motto, "Flooring New Mexico one project at a time," means that each customer—retail,

By fostering a familia-like atmosphere among his employees, founder Ray Lucero Sr. (middle, front) has built a business based on customized service, state-of-the-art products and techniques, and a personal guarantee to do the job right the first time.

Alan Weiner

Chuck Young

In 2002, as long-time Lobo fans, Ray's Flooring donated 100 percent of the labor and materials to redo the locker room floors for the men's and women's Lobo Basketball teams. (l-r): Ritchie McKay (men's head coach), Ray Lucero, Jr., Bernadette Frederick, Martin Lucero, Gerald Lucero, and Don Flanagan (women's head coach).

commercial, and builder—receives personal attention at every phase of the flooring project, whether that means a simple design consultation, a repair or refinishing project, or a major installation. With a staff of over twenty-five in sales and administration and another sixty-five working in installation, Ray's is able to serve the needs of clients throughout New Mexico, Arizona, Southern Colorado, and Texas. Products range from high-quality area rugs to glass block, to carpet, tile, vinyl, ceramic, brick, and wood flooring. All products are field proven in the commercial environment through testing and development by Ray's knowledgeable technical staff. Work is done by licensed and insured installers and comes with the Lucero family's guarantee to do the job right the first time.

As members of the New Mexico Floor Covering Association and the Flooring America Group, Ray's is always up-to-date on the latest products, styles, and techniques. "We use state-of-the-art technology to manage and increase productivity," says Lucero, Jr. "This allow us to be more efficient and it gives us an advantage over the competition." Ray's believes that the success in the industry will come from training our youth utilizing programs such as those offered by the Albuquerque Technical Vocational Institute. "Our goal is to grow throughout the Southwest and to get the best of the best to join us and help with this growth."

And, with seventeen grandchildren being raised among the Lucero children, odds are that growth will be led by strong family values for many years to come.♦

EACH YEAR IN APRIL THOUSANDS OF NATIVE AMERICANS from across the United States attend the Gathering of Nations, the largest powwow in all of North America. Held at the UNM Arena and open to the public, participants gather to dance, play music, socialize and educate visitors about Native American issues.

◄ **SOME OF THE COUNTRY'S** top Native American performers compete for top prizes in the pow-wow's singing, dancing and drumming competition. To Native Americans, dancing is both a form of prayer and a way of celebrating life.

Alan Weiner — All

► ESTABLISHED IN 1983 TO PROMOTE Native American culture, the Gathering of Nations sponsors educational programs aimed at helping its youth keep their traditions alive through each new generation.

Homes By Marie, Inc.

Over a dozen years ago, Marie Elizabeth "Betty" Blea left a twenty-year banking career with a single goal in mind—to build homes that met her stringent standards. "My vision of quality is a long-lasting, well-structured home," she explains. By incorporating quality amenities into distinctive contemporary southwestern designs, the name Homes By Marie has come to signify some of the finest homes in the area.

Like so many of Albuquerque's entrepreneurs, Blea went into business for herself because she saw a better way of doing things. "I got involved with a home during a fundraiser." she recalls. After leaving her position at the bank, obtaining her contractor's license, and constructing a home with another builder, Blea realized the best way to build her idea of a home was to do it on her own terms.

In the beginning, Blea gained a reputation as a builder of smaller homes with better amenities. And as her reputation for quality grew, so did the demand for her to build homes reaching into the six-figure category. "Now we are one of the top builders in Albuquerque," she says. "If someone wants a high-end home, our name is usually in there somewhere." Today amenities like wood windows, skylights, radiant heat, and other features, which are commonly classified as extras in construction, are considered standard features in every "Homes By Marie" home.

Still, Homes By Marie continues to cater to the middle-market client, building smaller homes with nice amenities. "Variety is what we are building now," Blea says. "We cater to the retired clients and to the up-and-coming families with children that want the nicer amenities."

Homes By Marie quality is found in details, in the living spaces both inside and out. Whether building a moderately priced or a multi-million-dollar home, Homes By Marie incorporates the finest amenities into every corner.

Tim Wright—Both

listening and understanding a homeowner's
lifestyle, Homes By Marie builds to suit any need. For
mealtimes, that can mean anything from a simple
breakfast nook with a view to an elegant formal dining room.

From moderately priced to multi-million-
dollar projects, every Homes By Marie home reflects
Betty Blea's trademark listening skills. "There's a
lot more to building a home than just the
construction," she says. "We really try to hear our
clients' needs and put their needs in the building.
Also a big part of custom home building is
answering client concerns afterwards—being there
to service your clients can make or break a
reputation."

Partner Charles "Breck" Breckenridge, who joined Blea in her second year of business, has
forged the firm's reputation for excellence on the job site as well. As supervisor of quality control,
Breck works closely with subcontractors and suppliers to ensure superior workmanship, from tiled
floor to beamed ceiling. Michelle Barba, "the smiling face in the office," completes a firm kept
intentionally small to further promote accessibility.

Over the years, clients have expressed their delight with both repeat business and reports of
exceptional resale numbers. But perhaps the greatest reward for Homes By Marie is seeing the
dreams of so many New Mexicans fulfilled by ownership of quality homes. ◆

Alan Weiner

◄ **YEARLY POWWOWS SUCH** as the Gathering of Nations provide representatives from over 700 tribes throughout Canada and the United States the opportunity not only to socialize, but to also discuss the issues facing today's Native peoples. New Mexico's nineteen tribal governments agree that one of their greatest challenges is balancing cultural preservation with economic growth.

▼ **LOCATED JUST NORTH OF** Albuquerque, Sandia is one of the state's most progressive pueblo tribes, thanks in part to its dynamic current governor, Stuwart Paisano. Only twenty-eight years old when first elected in 2000, Paisano inspires loyalty and respect with progressive and preservationist agendas. In 2003, he was able to win for his people 10,000 federally granted acres of sacred ancestral land along the front side of the Sandias while also breaking ground on a stunning new resort and golf course.

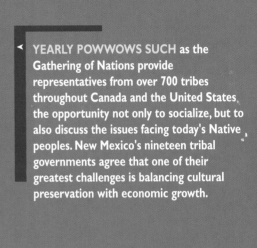

Rod Reilly

Geltmore, Inc.

Look around you. Chances are you're sitting in your home or office. You could also be in a bookstore, a hotel lobby, even a restaurant. But wherever you are, that space—the space that shelters you, entertains you, perhaps even inspires you—began as an idea in the mind of a developer.

In Albuquerque, that developer is likely to be Geltmore, Inc. Geltmore is the culmination of founder Paul Silverman's thirty-plus years of experience developing over 3 million square feet of industrial, offices, and retail property throughout the Southwest. As a result, Geltmore can meet a variety of client needs, whether that be a multi-use development like West Bluff Center at Coors and I-40, or a single-user structure like Sprint's call center in Rio Rancho.

As one of the few developers to have survived all five of New Mexico's real estate down cycles, Silverman also brings to Geltmore the ability to thrive in down markets. "Our depth of experience, understanding real estate cycles, the ability to create financial structures that withstand economic ebbs and flows, and a long-term ownership perspective is the basis of our success."

For eight years Silverman ran the business himself. Then in 1999 he was joined by attorney Suzie Lubar and, in 2001, by CPA Tracy Riffe. Together, the three make up a powerful team of visionaries, possessed of a persevering attitude founded on the belief that development can and should contribute to the vibrancy of a city.

"We strive to build highly productive work environments for the benefit of the working occupants, our customers and our investors," says Silverman. "In so doing, the local economy benefits, while at the same time we improve the built environment by leaving it better than we found it," he says.

The forty-seven-acre West Bluff Center was designed and built in the Northern New Mexican style, allowing it to compliment the visual aesthetics of the surrounding communities.

Chuck Young—Both

Ideally situated at Albuquerque's busiest intersection, the West Bluff Center at I-40 and Coors is Geltmore's largest Westside project to date, providing a 150,000-person trade area with everything from office and home building supplies to restaurants and retail clothing.

And they do it a little differently than most developers, which either build for a fee or build with the goal of selling upon completion. Instead, as an investment builder, Geltmore risks its own capital, time and energy in order to build and hold onto properties for the long term. "Our relationship with our customers is one of landlord and tenant," explains Silverman. "We build quality products in locations that have enduring value. Our dealings with our tenants, our customers, are based on long-term agreements that have to be fair to both parties."

By building the places where we live, work, eat and shop, the development industry can't help but have a tremendous impact upon our daily lives. Geltmore strives to make that impact a positive one. "Hopefully developers make enough money so that they too can live and work and play in the community," says Riffe. "But most exist for a more far-reaching goal. They want to have a positive impact upon the places where they live and raise their families. They want to see that old decrepit building or vacant lot turned into something productive and beautiful." ◆

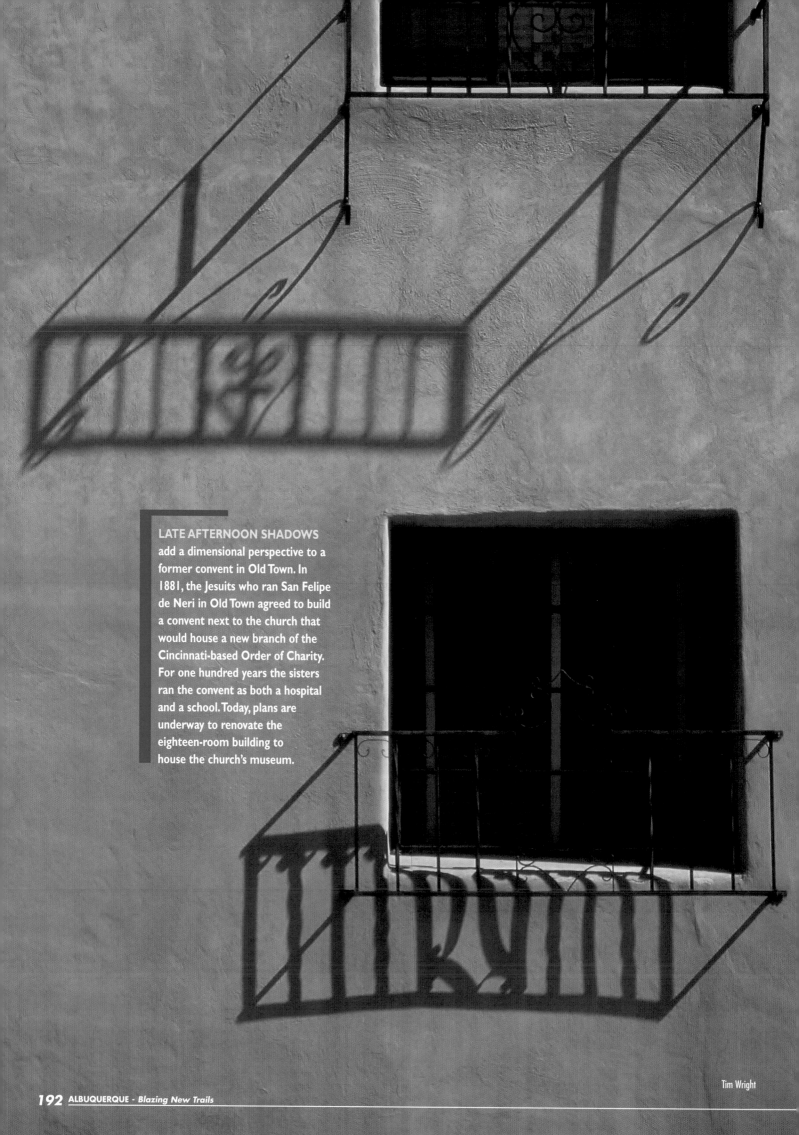

LATE AFTERNOON SHADOWS add a dimensional perspective to a former convent in Old Town. In 1881, the Jesuits who ran San Felipe de Neri in Old Town agreed to build a convent next to the church that would house a new branch of the Cincinnati-based Order of Charity. For one hundred years the sisters ran the convent as both a hospital and a school. Today, plans are underway to renovate the eighteen-room building to house the church's museum.

Tim Wright

Gerald Martin
General Contractor

From the legendary Rio Grande River to the peak of the Sandia Mountains, there isn't an area of Albuquerque upon which Gerald Martin General Contractor (GMGC) hasn't left its mark.

Established in 1974 by CEO Gerald Martin, who has been licensed in the state of New Mexico since 1955, the company has become the builder of choice among New Mexico's top business leaders. The result is such ambitious projects as the Sandia Peak Tramway, Sheraton Old Town Hotel, Hyatt Tamaya Destination Resort, the National Hispanic Cultural Center's Performing Arts Center, and the International Balloon Fiesta Museum.

What unifies these diverse projects is a commitment to excellence that is established long before breaking ground. "We engage in extensive pre-construction planning, and work our teams work diligently to communicate clear project goals to our network of subcontractors," says Executive Vice President Fred Gorenz.

This team-based approach provides clients with start-to-finish direction over their projects. Whether it's through design/build, design/assist or another contract method, GMCC consistently meets the client's budget and schedule goals while providing quality work in a safe environment.

The end result is "We don't just build buildings. People think our business is about bricks and mortar," says Matt Martin, President. "It isn't. It's about people and the relationships we build with them." As one long-time customer puts it, "They absolutely partner with the owners and operators of a project to ensure the best possible outcomes for all involved." ◆

Albuquerque's National Hispanic Cultural Center Performing Arts Complex shown near completion— another GMGC project "on time and within budget."

Gerald Martin General Contractors photo

ils

Rod Reilly

▲ **TO SCULPTOR KARL STALNAKER,** all the world's junk is his treasure as he combines such items as vintage auto parts, electrical appliances, tools, and lamp bases to create tongue-in-cheek sculptural commentaries on consumerism and the Machine Age.

◄ **SINCE 1977, WILLIAM STODDARD** of William Stoddard Construction, Inc. has designed and built some of the area's finest homes. His specialties include new construction, additions, and remodels. He is well known for his meticulous historical restorations on many of the oldest structures in New Mexico, such as the window and roof replacement on this 1935 WPA building that now serves as the law office of Steven Clark in Bosque Farms, New Mexico.

Coldwell Banker Legacy

In an ever-changing industry where emotions play a key role in buying decisions, one company understands the importance of really listening to customer needs. That focus is what makes Coldwell Banker Legacy New Mexico's number one real estate company. "Although the selling of homes is our medium," says Co-Chief Executive Officer Peter Parnegg, "we are really in the business of helping people through life transitions."

Coldwell Banker Legacy's roots date back to 1955 with the founding of H. Parnegg Realty, a firm that grew in size and reputation for four decades. In the 1980s, at about the same time Peter was taking over the family business from his father, Joe Gilmore and Michael Carter were forming their own competing agency, Metro 100. A decade later, the two companies combined to become Coldwell Banker Parnegg Metro Realtors, quickly rising to the lead in Albuquerque sales and closings.

Since that time, Peter, Mike and Joe have worked constantly to ensure that Coldwell Banker Legacy is known for delivering honest, accurate, uncomplicated results. Even under the best of circumstances, moving is challenging. The three often laugh when they say that if the agents do their job, people have to move! Knowing that at the end of the rainbow is a new house, the process can be made significantly less stressful by constant attention to detail mixed with a healthy dose of empathy.

Through hundreds of years of change and growth, Albuquerque remains the quintessential boomtown-optimistic, enterprising, and always striving to become the perfect place to call home.

Archival Shot

John Nugent

For sellers, Coldwell Banker Legacy has created a comprehensive, unique marketing program which includes print, internet, TV and a mall program to satisfy the marketing needs of its customers at an extraordinary level. The company believes that "Marketing Matters." If the customer can't find it, they can't buy it! The buyers of houses do not rely on agents selecting houses from MLS as their only information vehicle. Buyers do a lot of research themselves in this very consumer empowered age. Our marketing programs expose every one of our listings to the most number of buyers possible.

"We know that markets change, customers change, and customer needs change, says Gilmore. "And the better one is at listening and responding to that, the better one is likely to serve the customer." The cornerstone of that endeavor is simple - never assume. "People sometimes make enormous assumptions and then base all kinds of actions on those assumptions that they never verify," says Carter. "That's right at the core of what we are teaching our people, how to listen."

Since the turn of the new century, the firm has merged with and acquired additional agencies to become today's Coldwell Banker Legacy, an organization of ten offices, more than 500 agents, and nearly 40 percent of the market share.

In the midst of the challenge of the move, our goal is to make one destination for all their moving-related needs. To that end, we put a mortgage company, a title company and concierge department, all under one roof. In addition to finding you a house, you can get the loan to buy the house and get the vendors to fix anything that needs to be fixed or improved, all in one stop. ◆

THERE'S NO CHANCE OF SANTA
missing Albuquerque when he makes
his rounds on Christmas Eve. Each
holiday season families throughout
the city turn heads and warm hearts
as they transform their homes into
elaborate displays of color and light.

John Nugent

Wyndham Albuquerque Hotel

From its airport location overlooking the city, the Wyndham Albuquerque Hotel offers a uniquely different view of airport hotels. Certainly, complimentary twenty-four-hour airport transportation, as well as proximity to the interstate and the city's business district, makes staying at the Wyndham convenient for travelers. But what is truly special about this airport property is its exceptional guest service, imparted by a staff with a naturally ingrained sense of incomparable hospitality. "The standard we set here at the Wyndham is that the guest is our number one priority," explains Assistant General Manager Cynthia Fresquez. "Guests are always welcomed upon arrival, and thanked upon departure, and someone is always there to serve. There is also an overall sense of consistency because some of our staff have been here as long as the property's been here?they've worked together for so long, they know what the expectations are."

Guests appreciate knowing what to expect at the Wyndham. Beyond the overall friendliness and familiarity of the staff, guests stay in first-class accommodations with standard amenities ranging from coffee makers to data ports. Special amenities are a part of every room in the Wyndham Club Level, which also offers relaxation in the Vista Grande Lounge. For working travelers, there is a fully equipped business center, and for those who enjoy a little recreation, choices range from a relaxing pool to outdoor jogging trails. Through the unique Wyndham ByRequest program, guests can expect not only express service, but also additional amenities customized to particular needs.

It's not long before guests realize this isn't your average airport hotel. Extraordinary hospitality, top-notch amenities, and customized service make the Wyndham a consistent choice among business and pleasure travelers alike.

Chuck Young—Both

WYNDHAM

Although its name and artist have long been forgotten, this stone-carved guardian serves as a symbol of welcome to those who make the Wyndham their home away from home.

The Wyndham's exceptional dining venues are another atypical aspect of this airport property. "Only the highest quality can be expected of the Wyndham culinary team," says Food and Beverage Director Davilay Wells, revealing the main ingredient to any Wyndham service. "We simply try to take great care of our guests the first time, since they are usually with us for a short period of time. This level of service makes our guests feel comfortable and willing to tell others about their stay and the experience they had." While the Rojo Grill offers a delectable menu for breakfast, lunch, and dinner, the Rojo Lounge features comfortable seating for spirits and relaxation.

As a full-service property, the Wyndham also offers flexible meeting space, technology, and planning support for groups of up to one thousand. "Nothing is too big or too small for this team," says Wells. Whether it is a simple get together or a national convention, the Wyndham and its staff can provide for every detail.

The Wyndham's elevated service standards produce consistently high occupancy rates and repeated recognition in industry rating systems, evidence that the Wyndham Albuquerque Hotel is far more than a typical airport property, it is a prime example of extraordinary hospitality. ◆

CREATED FROM TILE AND MASSIVE blocks of stone, the fountain in Albuquerque's Civic Plaza is both a monumental work of public art and a welcome oasis in the middle of the city.

Tim Wright — All

ONE OF LOCAL artists Glenna Goodacre's statues echoes in bronze the dozens of real-life children who each day during the summer flock to the Plaza with their families.

TEMPTING AS IT IS to wade in, the wide pools that surround the fountain are purely ornamental. But visitors are more than welcome to toss in a coin or two for luck, or, like this young man, at least contemplate their reflection in the pool's shimmering surface.

DoubleTree Hotel Albuquerque

From the scent of warm chocolate chip cookies wafting in the air, guests know the moment they enter the DoubleTree Hotel Albuquerque that they are leaving the hassles of the road behind. "We prefer a much warmer and personal experience, and we try to do everything we can to ensure guest satisfaction and comfort," says General Manager Bob Gansfuss. "And as a result, we are viewed as a high quality, upscale hotel, whose principal competitive strength is our ability to make guests feel at home."

That same down-to-earth approach permeates every aspect of the DoubleTree, making it Albuquerque's preferred downtown location. Whether it is a corporate gathering, luncheon meeting, or special occasion, guests of the DoubleTree can expect the same congenial treatment in every venue.

When it comes to business, the DoubleTree's downtown location and meeting amenities also make it the perfect place for gatherings of any size. In addition to its own 6,000 square feet of space, the hotel is located adjacent to the convention center, a block away from the Wool Warehouse Theatre, and convenient to all major commercial centers and attractions.

The DoubleTree also features exceptional dining options here in the heart of Albuquerque. "We offer excellent grand continental menu items that our guests will recognize and enjoy, and our Southwestern offerings are designed to bring an exciting new experience to our guests who have not been exposed to our unique and addicting cuisine," says Food & Beverage Director Michael Weig. Open for breakfast, lunch, and dinner, the DoubleTree's La Cascada restaurant features delectable items like cast-iron seared Pueblo Beef Tenderloin, Poblano Chile Rellenos, and a signature Green Chile Stew.

With its southwestern-style wooden accents, colorful murals, and indigenous artworks, the DoubleTree's lobby reflects the overall spirit of the hotel: upscale yet at the same time warm and inviting.

Chuck Young—Both

Providing exemplary hospitality in the heart of downtown, the DoubleTree Hotel is located adjacent to the Convention Center and just minutes from theatres, shopping, restaurants, and commercial and government centers.

Such mouthwatering selections, combined with a professional staff of meeting and convention planners, have earned the DoubleTree a reputation as a local leader in the social catering market. From a formal banquet for hundreds of guests to an intimate setting for close family and friends, the DoubleTree can customize menus to create the most appropriate atmosphere and make every event an unforgettable occasion. Among its unique menu designs are a variety of food stations throughout the room to encourage guests to mingle rather than remain in a centralized area.

When the people of Albuquerque voice their special needs, the DoubleTree shows its community spirit by answering the call. "We get many requests for local donations and we try to honor as many of them as possible, because this is our home," says Gansfuss. DoubleTree donations and auction items help raise funds for groups and organizations that benefit the entire community. And as its community prospers, the DoubleTree Hotel Albuquerque will continue to anchor this city's center with genuine spirit of hospitality. ◆

LOCAL PUNK ROCK BAND HOBBES FURY plays an alcohol-free gig at a popular downtown nightclub, the Launchpad. Albuquerque supports a vibrant live music scene, with the majority of the clubs located along Central Avenue, from the University to downtown.

Chuck Young

Albuquerque Marriott Pyramid North

S ince 1986 travelers from balloonists to businessmen have counted on the Albuquerque Marriott Pyramid North hotel to offer superior service and amenities in an elegant and relaxing atmosphere. Formerly the Crowne Plaza Pyramid, this John Q. Hammon-owned hotel changed flags in late 2002, bringing with it the dedication and experience that has made them the first name in hospitality. Each guest receives VIP-style attention as outlined in the Pyramid's in-house "At Your Service" philosophy and the Marriott's "20 Basics" of hospitality, all based on the idea that Marriott doesn't sell rooms, it sells service.

Conveniently located minutes from the airport at the northern end of Albuquerque, the Marriott Pyramid North is the focal point of the Journal Center, Albuquerque's most modern industrial and business complex. All the city's popular sights are close by as well, including downtown, Old Town, the University of New Mexico, historical centers, casinos, and museums. In addition, its proximity to the Albuquerque International Balloon Fiesta Park makes it the number one choice of balloonists and spectators who attend this spectacular yearly event.

The Pyramid's Aztec-style exterior is reflected in its interior with a magnificent ten-story atrium surrounding the hotel's lobby.

Chuck Young—All

Many guests end a busy day of sightseeing or business meetings with a relaxing drink outside the Pyramid's High Desert Lounge, where they can enjoy the soothing sounds of the nearby fifty-foot waterfall.

Room phones have only two buttons: a message retrieval button and the "At Your Service" button. At the other end of this line is the go-to person for everything from room and laundry service to housekeeping and transportation.

continued on page 210

The exterior design of the hotel mimics an Aztec temple, making it one of the city's most distinctive buildings. After passing through the elegant Santa Fe southwestern-style lobby, guests enter a soaring ten-story atrium augmented by lush greenery and the soothing sounds of a rock waterfall. Each of the hotel's 252 rooms and sixty-two suites feature amenities for both business and pleasure travelers, including dual line telephones with data ports and voice mail, high-speed internet access, an oversized work desk, ironing board and iron, hair dryer, coffee maker and a complimentary USA Today delivered each morning. The hotel also features a business center, gift shop, and concierge level.

Founder John Q. Hammons commissioned architect Jack Hood to design the Marriott Pyramid as a building with an unusual and distinct silhouette that would serve as a stimulus for other businesses to locate to the area.

continued from page 209

For those wishing to keep fit, the Pyramid offers a fully equipped exercise room, an indoor/outdoor pool, spas, and a sauna. Golf, tennis facilities, and a jogging path are close by, as is top-notch skiing at Sandia Peak, thirty minutes away by tram.

With over 27,000 square feet of meeting space and the most current audiovisual and teleconferencing technology, the Pyramid can easily accommodate groups up to 1,600 people. In addition, a 12,000-square-foot ballroom makes the hotel an elegant location for weddings, anniversaries, graduations, and birthday parties. A professional catering and events planning staff is on hand to help coordinate and run any affair.

In keeping with Marriott's high standards in food service, guests can enjoy the Red Sky Cafè—a charming restaurant tucked in the lush greenery of the atrium for breakfast and lunch. For those interested in dinner, the Sandia Grille, offers both American favorites and local New Mexican specialties. For a quick breakfast, lunch or dinner, room service is also available from 5 A.M. to 11 P.M. daily. Those wishing to spend a night out on the town are surrounded by some of the finest nightlife in the city, including the on-site High Desert Lounge.

As a long-time member of the community the Pyramid is active in numerous local and national business associations and also hosts several charitable events. In 2003, the hotel hosted its first annual Halloween party, called the "the Boo Ball." The ball will offer philanthropic- minded adults the chance to dress up and party down, all the while raising funds for a variety of worthy causes. ◆

First impressions are everything: from the moment guests arrive, they know to expect the best in southwestern style, comfort, and service.

WITH THEIR FIVE FLYING STAR RESTAURANT locations, owners Jean and Mark Bernstein have created a mini culinary empire, in which funky diner meets high-class restaurant. Patrons are drawn to the fresh, imaginatively prepared food, mouth-watering pastries, eclectic décor, and dog-friendly outdoor patios.

Charles Ledford

Wool Warehouse

When flocks of sheep began dotting the New Mexican landscape in the seventeenth century, they signified the onset of an industry that would bring prosperity to the people of Albuquerque. Today, the Wool Warehouse is the sole symbol of that heritage, standing as an elegant tribute to a city's history.

Designed by T. Charles Gaastra and owned by wool merchant Frank Bond, the Wool Warehouse operated for more than thirty years before the industry's decline. When wool no longer passed through its doors, the warehouse was used for city storage until its transformation into an entertainment venue.

As a dinner theatre, the impressive brick and columned structure held great promise for a number of years. But despite its beauty, the Wool Warehouse struggled to remain profitable, finally becoming the property of Youth Development, Inc. (YDI), a non-profit group providing programs for residents in need.

In support of this group's efforts, the DoubleTree has brought new life to the space, using its theatre stage and seating, restaurant, and gallery spaces for exciting events and gatherings. From awards ceremonies to business seminars, the Wool Warehouse offers a unique downtown space for a variety of uses. Furthermore, the DoubleTree donates a portion of the warehouse revenues back to YDI.

Listed on the National Register of Historic Places, the Wool Warehouse has once again become a bustling center of activity and a standing tribute to a city's heritage. ◆

The elegant Art Deco-inspired ballroom of this 1929 architectural landmark accommodates up to 500 people, making it the perfect choice for weddings, award ceremonies, conferences and special events.

Charles Ledford

LIKE DINOSAURS? The New Mexico Museum of Natural History and Science in New Mexico is the place to be, with its life-sized sculptures of over a dozen different dinosaurs and close up glimpses of real life remnants in the FossilWorks room.

Chuck Young

Eclipse Aviation Corporation

Eclipse Aviation is out to change the way people travel. Founded by aviation enthusiast and former Microsoft executive Vern Raburn, the Eclipse team of over two hundred engineers, pilots, inventors, and paradigm busters is poised to revolutionize the personal transportation industry. And they're doing it not by starting a new airline, but by building an entirely new airplane.

As president and CEO of Eclipse Aviation, Raburn's vision is to build a jet aircraft aimed at the growing market of travelers who are no longer efficiently served by the airline industry's hub and spoke system, in which 67 percent of American travelers are routed through only about twenty-nine out of ten thousand airports. That's fine for long distance and coast-to-coast journeys but it can cause tremendous gridlock for those needing to fly quickly and directly over shorter distances, say, Albuquerque to Austin or Wichita to Washington.

Enter the Eclipse 500, a six-place, twin turbofan jet that is safer, easier to operate, and more cost-efficient than any jet aircraft on the market. And the Eclipse 500 provides high-tech features once available only on the most modern airliners and high-end business jets for about $1 million. Those characteristics have made the Eclipse 500 the ideal aircraft for companies launching a new service, the "air taxi," where the plane waits for the passenger instead of the other way around.

"Our plane isn't intended to do what the airlines do best - high volume, long distance flying. The best analogy I have is personal computers. They didn't put large mainframes out of business. To the contrary, PCs created new uses, new reasons for computing. So our plane is an alternative-explicitly designed to function out of the other nine thousand or so airports the big airlines don't use," says Raburn.

Housing the engineering, administration, and flight test divisions, Eclipse company headquarters at Clark Carr Loop SE is one of three Albuquerque-based facilities.

Rod Reilly—All

ECLIPSE 500

N500E

Engineers Ray Woodson and Julie Pruitt are part of the team that is building a jet aircraft that will change the way Americans travel.

By using friction stir welding (an innovative joining process that replaces 60 percent of the rivets normally used on major aircraft assemblies), precisely machined parts, and a modular approach to assembly, Eclipse will significantly reduce the labor required to build the Eclipse 500. This means high production rates, which are estimated to exceed 1,000 a year at full production. At that time, Eclipse also hopes to have moved from its current manufacturing site at the Albuquerque International Sunport to the Double Eagle II Airport, located on the city's West Side.

Albuquerque was chosen as the company's base of operations after beating out sixty-two other candidates, including Phoenix and Salt Lake City, because of its great economic package and almost year-round perfect flying weather. In turn, Eclipse will be a tremendous boon to Albuquerque's economy. Already the company has created around two hundred jobs and business

continued on page 216

Brett Barker, team lead for the assembly department, prepares the first Eclipse 500 for flight testing.

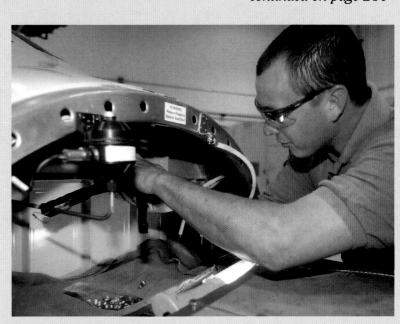

Rod Reilly

Utilizing computer analytical techniques, design engineer Damon Phillips and mechanical design engineer Chris Box (l-r) design and evaluate components and subassemblies of the Eclipse 500 aircraft.

continued from page 215

leaders hope that number will rise to over two thousand. And, even at this early stage, Raburn encourages his employees to participate in their community at both the corporate and individual level. Once a quarter, the company picks a local cause to which they donate their time and energy. "What we lack in money, we make up in time and effort," he says. "It's just being a good corporate citizen."

In manufacturing and technology businesses, the journey from conception to inception can be a long and arduous one but Raburn believes he is better positioned to buck the odds than most. In addition to having spent his entire career in the technology businesses (he was Microsoft's eighteenth hire), he also possesses the entrepreneurial ability to think big.

Sponsor Supplied

"Starting an airplane business is something that hasn't been done in about forty years," he says. "But, there's a real need for it and the technologies are there." Those who take the chance and navigate the perils of that universe oftentimes end up changing lives for the better. If Eclipse's orders—which currently sit at just over two thousand—are any indication, it may not be long before many of us are moving about the country with greater speed and efficiency than ever before. ◆

Team lead David Reed and program manager Kathryn Ray (l-r) were two of eight Eclipse employees who participated in Albuquerque's 2003 School to World program. The program, in which eighth and ninth graders learn about business and industry management, represents the kind of hands-on volunteerism encouraged at Eclipse.

Built to out-perform and out-price other jets in its class, the six-seat, $1 million Eclipse 500 will cruise at 375 knots at an altitude of 41,000 feet with a range of 1,280 nautical miles.

Sponsor Supplied

THOSE WHO LOVE COMMUNITY THEATRE can work behind the scenes as well. Each Albuquerque Little Theatre production involves over five hundred volunteers. Also, an open-casting policy welcomes old hands and newcomers alike, so there's always a new face or two at every show.

Chuck Young — Both

Rose's Southwest Papers

Starting a business can be a daunting task even under ideal circumstances. For foreigners totally unfamiliar with the business environment of their adopted country, the effort can seem insurmountable. Still, when Roberto and Rose Marie Espat immigrated to the United States in 1981, they didn't think about the problems, only the solutions.

It was their wish to expand the successful paper conversion business they'd established in their native Belize in 1972, but as that region's political and economic climate worsened, the Espats realized they'd have to leave in order to do so.

After much research, the Espats chose Albuquerque as their new home. In 1984 they opened a business selling toilet paper and paper towels to home consumers. Business boomed and a year later they built their own twenty-thousand-square-foot manufacturing center in the southwest neighborhood of Barelas.

After receiving their first major contract from the General Services Administration, the Espats decided to shift their focus to manufacturing and distributing paper products for commercial and fast food industries. The decision proved to be a fortuitous one. Eventually they signed exclusive contracts with McDonald's and Burger King as well.

The next time you sit down to a meal from McDonald's or Burger King, take a look at your napkin. Chances are, it was produced in Roses' napkin conversion division, which runs twenty-four hours a day, seven days a week.

Roses aim is to produce products of the highest quality on a timely and cost-effective manner. Sales are made by truckload quantities only and are shipped nationwide. Based on purchase orders received, Roses products are produced, palletized, stacked, and stored until shipped. The turn around time on orders is typically two weeks.

Today the company's sixteen conversion machines run twenty-four-hours a day, seven days a week, transforming jumbo rolls of raw paper product into hundreds of millions of paper bags, paper towels, toilet paper, napkins, and tissues that are shipped to customers throughout the nation. Always on the lookout for ways to save their customers time and money, Roses also provides one-stop services that include custom converting, packaging, and private labeling.

Presently, Roses purchases its raw materials from outside sources, but plans are underway to become fully integrated within the next few years by adding a recycling and de-inking plant and a paper mill. This will not only save millions of dollars from outsourcing their raw materials, but the Espats anticipate the expansion will create another 150-200 jobs.

Growing up, Roberto and Rose Marie were taught that success was based on hard work, determination, and, above all, integrity. In turn, they passed these values on to their own children and other relatives, many of whom now work for the company.

continued on page 222

Roberto Espat (l) founded Roses on the premise that good business is based on honesty, dignity, and fairness. Today, his son, Vice President Robert Espat, Jr, (r), ensures that legacy continues in all facets of the operation.

continued from page 221

Their son, Executive Vice President Robert Espat, says that these values form their entire business culture. "Our family, team, and ethical approach to everything we do results in a lack of bureaucracy, lower overhead costs, and higher efficiencies. Every relationship that Roses is involved in, whether it's with suppliers, customers, or personnel, we always assure ourselves that the question, 'Is it fair to all involved?' is asked and answered affirmatively."

As a result, Roses has become one of the most respected family owned businesses in the state, having received a slew of accolades from local and national business organizations. In 2002, Roses Southwest Papers was ranked 96 in the Hispanic Business Magazine's top 500 largest Hispanic-owned companies in the United States. In addition, Robert Espat was awarded New Mexico's Small Business Person of the Year award for 2002. In 2001, Roses was honored to be ranked 35 in the Inc. Magazine's Inner City 100 list of the fastest growing private companies located in America's inner cities

In fact, inner-city revitalization is very important to Roberto and Rose Marie. Not only do they live and work downtown, but Roberto also serves on the board of the Barelas Community Development Corporation, an organization dedicated to revitalizing one of the city's oldest downtown neighborhoods.

Like so many immigrants before them, Roberto and Rose Marie Espat came to the United States hoping to create a better life for their family, and have succeeded. In the process, they also helped to improve the quality of life for a large portion of Albuquerque as well. ◆

State-of-the-art tissue and towel conversion machines produce bathroom, facial, and jumbo roll tissue, as well as a variety of commercial use towel. Like all Roses products, they are made from 100 percent recycled materials and starch based glues.

John Nugent

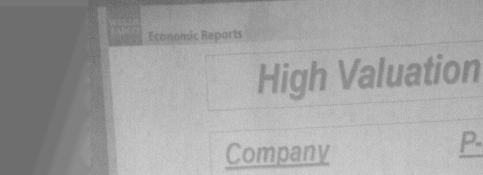

THE MARRIOTT PYRAMID NORTH HOTEL DISTINGUISHES ITSELF IN MANY AREAS
of customer service, not the least of which is its ability to accommodate large conferences
and events. With 27,000 square feet of meeting space and state-of-the-art audiovisual and
teleconferencing technology, Pyramid is a top choice for businesses and organizations
throughout the state and the nation.

Technology Ventures Corporation

N ew ideas and new technology have led to New Mexico's new economy. It is an economy that has been formed by vision and leadership. For the last ten years, the partnership between Sandia and Technology Ventures Corporation has helped to generate New Mexico's new economy by supporting the formation of high-tech businesses.

The results can be seen in the thousands of high-paying jobs that have been created at dozens of new companies. Then there are the fifteen seed and venture funds that have opened offices in New Mexico. They have contributed to the hundreds of millions of investment dollars that have been attracted to the state by the new economy.

This economy has led to Albuquerque being recently rated number one in the nation for high tech real output growth by the Milken Institute. More growth is on the way. The new economy can be seen at work in the Sandia Science and Technology Park, a place for high-tech companies to work together in close proximity to Sandia's resources.

The new economy. It is here now. The partnership of TVC and Sandia has helped make it happen. And it means a brighter future for us all. ◆

Dr. C. Paul Robinson, director, Sandia National Laboratories, and Sherman McCorkle, president and CEO, Technology Ventures Corporation.

Technology Ventures photo

EACH YEAR IN FALL, DOZENS of iron-barreled chile roasters make their appearance on curbsides across the city. Productive operations, like this one in front of the Farmer's Market at Stanford and Lead, can roast up to 1,200 pounds a day. Chile lovers who miss the September through October season could be out of luck— each year there's an increase in worldwide demand for New Mexico's smoky-flavored crop.

im Wright

THE TWO MISSIONS AGAINST JAPAN

THREE NEW MEXICANS who played important roles in the development of modern weaponry—(L-r) Ret. Navy Chief Warrant Gunner and primary project officer for the W76 Trident Missile, Charles O. Schmidt; Ret. Air Force Senior Master Sergeant with the Manhattan Project, Ganarld "Gerry" Taylor; and Senior Mentor to Sandia National Laboratories' Weapon Intern Program, Tom Schultheis—pose in front of a replica of the "Fat Man" atomic bomb, housed at the National Atomic Museum downtown. Today, the men serve as docents for the museum, established in 1969 as the only congressionally chartered museum of nuclear science and history, that tells the story of the Atomic Age from early research through today's uses of nuclear technology.

Chuck Young

A FAMILIAR SIGHT TO FREQUENT PLAYERS ARE PAA-KO'S
superintendent Rob Murray and his trusty Labrador Murphy as they make
their daily rounds, offering tips, encouragement and a friendly woof or
two. Paa-Ko's personable and knowledgeable staff is 100 percent dedicated
to making each and every golfers experience a memorable one.

CURRENTLY RANKED BEST GOLF COURSE IN NEW MEXICO
by *Golf Digest* and among the top one hundred courses in the
country by *Golf Magazine*, Paa-Ko Ridge is a public course with all
the amenities of a private club. Situated along the gently rolling
eastern slopes of the Sandia Mountains, the course was designed to
incorporate the features and terrain of the surrounding landscape,
creating a course that is both visually stunning and challenging to
golfers at all skill levels.

Tim Wright — Both

WHETHER SKIING THE SLOPES of the Sandias, hiking the foothills, biking a nature trail along the river or, like this young fellow, sliding down The Scream Body Slide at the Beach Water Park, Albuquerqueans are able to enjoy the great outdoors all year.

John Nugent

Featured Companies

Albuquerque Hispano Chamber of Commerce

1309 Fourth Street, NW
Albuquerque, NM 87102
Phone: (505) 842-9003
Fax: (505) 764-8829
www.ahcmn.org

The activities of the Albuquerque Hispano Chamber of Commerce foster economic development through business opportunity, workforce education, tourism promotion, and legislative advocacy.

Category:
Chamber of Commerce

pp. 92-93

Albuquerque International Balloon Fiesta

4401 Alameda Boulevard N.E.
Albuquerque, NM 87113
Phone: (505) 821-1000
Fax: (505) 828-2887
www.balloonfiesta.com
balloons@balloonfiesta.com

A sight to behold in the air and on the ground, the annual Albuquerque International Balloon Fiesta draws hundreds of thousands for over a week of flight, food, and above all, fun.

Category:
Community Enrichment

p. 157

Albuquerque Marriott Pyramid North

5151 San Francisco Road
Northeast
Albuquerque, NM 87109
Phone: (505) 821-3333
Fax: (505) 822-8115
www.marriott.com\abqmc

Distinctive architectural styling and Marriott's attention to service and amenities, make this one of Albuquerque's most popular hotels.

Category: Hotel

pp. 208-210

Bank of Albuquerque, NA

P.O. Box 26148
Albuquerque, NM 87125
(800) 583-0709 ExpressBank
(888) 424-3578 Operator
(505) 855-7239 Fax (Public Relations)
www.bankofalbuquerque.com

By understanding and focusing on local markets and community dynamics, Bank of Albuquerque delivers world-class products and services with a decidedly personalized touch.

Category:
Financial Services

pp. 50-51

Bank of America

P.O. Box 25500
Albuquerque, NM 87125
Phone: (505) 282-4010
Fax: (505) 282-4664
www.bankofamerica.com

People, convenience, choice, and support of the local community, these are the products and services offered by the Albuquerque branches of Bank of America.

Category:
Financial Services

p.47

Bernalillo County

County Manager's Office
One Civic Plaza Northwest,
10th Floor
Albuquerque, NM 87102
Phone: (505) 768-4000
Fax: (505) 768-4329
www.bernco.gov

By seeking out partnerships with private sector industries, Bernalillo County has strengthened its ability to provide financial stability, economic growth, and a better quality of life for its residents.

Category: County
Government

p. 76-77

Blue Cross and Blue Shield of New Mexico

P.O. Box 27630
Albuquerque, NM 87125
Phone: (505) 291-3500
or (800) 835-8699
www.bcbsnm.com

Blue Cross and Blue Shield of New Mexico offers a full continuum of health insurance benefit plans for groups and individuals.

Category: Healthcare

pp. 154-155

Burt & Nagel, CPA's, LLC

4001 Indian School Road NE,
Suite 321
Albuquerque, NM 87110
Phone: (505) 265-6604
Fax: (505) 268-9931
www.bncpa.com
bncpa@bncpa.com

Burt & Nagel, CPA's count success by its ability to strengthen the community through services that help businesses and not-for-profit organizations succeed and enhance the quality of life for the people of Albuquerque.

Category: CPA firm

pp. 24-26

Cardinal Health/Allegiance Healthcare

4200 Osuna Road NE
Albuquerque, NM 87109
Phone: (505) 761-1000
Fax: (505) 761-1776
www.cardinal.com

A division of Cardinal Health, Financial Shared Services Center of Allegiance Healthcare in Albuquerque is dedicated to helping health care providers fulfill their mission of caring for patients.

Category:
Healthcare Service

pp. 134-135

Charter Building and Development Corporation

11000 Spain Road, Northeast
Building B
Albuquerque, NM 87111
Phone: (505) 275-4360
Fax: (505) 275-5656
www.charterhome.com
sales@charterhome.com

As a partner in the Building America Program, Charter Building and Development Corporation is building communities with greater efficiency, cleaner air, and more comfort.

Category:
General Contractor

pp. 170-172

Citibank

9521 San Mateo NE
Albuquerque, NM 87113
Phone: (505) 797-6100
Fax: (505) 797-6250
www.citicards.com

Citibank, a member of Citigroup, has a twenty-year history in Albuquerque and employs more than 1,300 people in credit card telephone support services.

Category:
Financial Services

p.33

Coldwell Banker Legacy

6725 Academy Road NE
Albuquerque, NM 87109
Phone: (505) 857-2222
Fax: (505) 857-2343
www.cblegacynm.com

Coldwell Banker Legacy is a residential realty organization with ten offices, more than 500 agents, and nearly 40 percent of the market share.

Category:
Residential Realtor

pp. 196-197

DoubleTree Hotel Albuquerque

201 Marquette NW
Albuquerque, NM 87102
Phone: (505) 247-3344
Fax: (505) 247-7025
www.doubletreealbuquerque.com

In the center of it all, the DoubleTree Hotel Albuquerque is the downtown place for accommodations, meetings, and dining.

Category: Hotel

pp. 204-205

Downtown Action Team & Historic Downtown Improvement Company

c/o Griffin & Associates
924 Park Avenue SW, Suite E
Albuquerque, NM 87102
Phone: (505) 764-4444
Fax: (505) 764-8636
bmorris@swcp.com

These two societies have contributed immensely to the revitalization of Albuquerque's downtown, which is rapidly becoming the city's business, entertainment, and cultural hub.

Category: Non-profit

pp. 70-73

Eclipse Aviation Corporation

2503 Clark Carr Loop SE
Albuquerque, NM 87106
Phone: (505) 245-7555
Fax: (505) 245-7888
www.eclipseaviation.com

Eclipse Aviation is ushering in a fresh age of aviation by producing a new jet aircraft that gives travelers the opportunity to move about the country with greater efficiency.

Category: Aviation

pp. 214-217

Enterprise Builders Corporation

8316 Washington NE
Albuquerque, NM 87113
Phone: (505) 857-0050
Fax: (505) 857-0054
www.entbldrs.com

With a sense of fair play and dedication to quality, Enterprise Builders has successfully completed over two thousand construction projects throughout New Mexico.

Category:
Building and Development

p. 175

Ever-Ready Oil Company and Redi Mart

3200 Broadway Blvd SE
Albuquerque, NM 87105
Phone: (505) 842-6121
Fax: (505) 247-3918

From its Depression Era beginnings, to its modern day position as one of New Mexico's largest fuel distribution companies, Ever-Ready Oil has remained true to its core values of honesty, respect, and personalized customer service.

Category: Fuel Distributor

p. 160

Eye Associates of New Mexico, Ltd.

Administrative Office
8801 Horizon Boulevard
Albuquerque, NM 87113
Phone: (505) 768-1339
Fax: (505) 244-9566
www.eyenm.com

Eye Associates is the Southwest's preeminent eye-care practice, offering the full range of care from general examinations to subspecialty expertise for the most complex diseases.

Category:
Eye Care Practice

pp. 148-151

First State Bank (First State Bancorporation)

7900 Jefferson NE
Albuquerque, NM 87109
Phone: (505) 241-7500
www.fsbnm.com

First State Bank, the wholly owned subsidiary of the locally managed First State Bancorporation, serves customers from twenty-three statewide branches.

Category:
Financial Services

pp. 40-42

Gap Inc.

40 First Plaza
Albuquerque, NM 87102
Phone: (866) 411-2772
www.gapinc.com

The mission of Gap Inc.'s Corporate Shared Service Center is to deliver world-class financial operations and support services to Gap Inc.'s global business partners and employees.

Category: Financial and Human Resources

p.35

Geltmore, Inc.

4408 Canyon Court NE
Albuquerque, NM 87111
Phone: (505) 294-8625
Fax: (505) 294-2225
paul.silverman@geltmore.com

Backed by experience, innovation and dedication, a Geltmore development is an investment in Albuquerque for the long term.

Category:
General Contractor

pp. 190-191

Gerald Martin
General Contractor

8501 Jefferson Street NE
Albuquerque, NM 87113
Phone: 505-828-1144
Fax: 505-828-9491
www.geraldmartin.com

Specializing in commercial and industrial construction projects, Gerald Martin is the contractor of choice for many of New Mexico's most respected business and community leaders.

Category:
General Contractor

p. 193

Grant Thornton LLP

6501 Americas Parkway
Northeast, Suite 565
Albuquerque, NM 87110
Phone: (505) 855-7900
Fax: (505) 855-7938
www.grantthornton.com

Grant Thornton is the leading global accounting, tax and business advisory firm dedicated to serving the needs of middle-market companies. Founded in 1924, Grant Thornton serves public and private middle-market clients through 51 offices in the United States and in 585 offices in 110 countries through Grant Thornton International.

Category:
Financial Services

pp. 114-115

Greater Albuquerque
Chamber of
Commerce

115 Gold S.W.
Suite 201
Albuquerque, NM 87102
Phone: (505) 764-3700
Fax: (505) 764-3714
www.gacc.org

The members of the Greater Albuquerque Chamber of Commerce take an active role in identifying metropolitan area needs and fostering a healthy business climate through economic growth.

Category:
Chamber of Commerce

pp.88-89

Griffin & Associates

924 Park Avenue SW, Suite E
Albuquerque, NM 87102
Phone: (505) 764-4444
Fax: (505) 764-8636
www.griffinassoc.com
info@griffinassoc.com

Clients throughout the Southwest rely on the innovative team at Griffin & Associates to produce dynamic public relations and marketing campaigns that get noticed and get results.

Category: Public Relations
and Marketing

pp.100-101

Goodwill Industries
of New Mexico

5000 San Mateo Northeast
Albuquerque, NM 87109
Phone: (505) 881-6401
Fax: (505) 884-3157
www.goodwillnm.org

Every year, Goodwill Industries of New Mexico helps thousands of people with disabilities and life challenges overcome employment hurdles through training programs that are funded by retail sales and an online auction of donated items.

Category: Non-profit

pp 28-29

Heart Hospital
of New Mexico

504 Elm Street NE
Albuquerque, NM 87102
Phone: (505) 724-2000
Fax: (505) 246-9933
www.hearthospitalnm.com

This innovative, physician-directed specialty hospital concentrates on the diagnosis and treatment of heart disease by establishing an efficient, patient and family centered care environment.

Category: Hospital

pp. 138-141

Homes By Marie, Inc.

P.O. Box 2777
Corrales, NM 87048
Phone: (505) 342-1532
Fax: (505) 342-1579
www.homesbymarie.com
marie@homesbymarie.com

Homes By Marie is a builder of quality homes with exceptional standard features in contemporary southwestern designs.

Category:
Building and Development

pp. 186-187

John F. Nugent Photography

128 Riata Trail SE
Rio Rancho, NM 87124
Phone: (505) 892-3345
Fax: (505) 896-2227
www.jfnphoto.com
jfnphoto@hotmail.com

John F. Nugent creates imaginative photos that capture the spirit of the moment. His expertise ranges from portraits to weddings to journalism to commercial photography.

Category: Photography

pp. 118-119

KPMG LLP

6565 Americas Parkway NE,
Suite 700
Albuquerque, NM 87110
Phone: (505) 884-3939
Fax: (505) 884-8348
www.us.kpmg.com

KPMG LLP provides accounting, auditing, and tax services to clients in Albuquerque and surrounding states.

Category: Accounting Firm

p.105

Modrall Sperling

500 Fourth Street Northwest
Bank of America Center,
Suite 1000
Albuquerque, NM 87102
Phone: (505) 848-1800
Fax: (505) 848-1882
www.modrall.com

Modrall Sperling provides legal counsel and representation for individuals and businesses throughout New Mexico and the Southwest.

Category: Legal Counsel

pp. 110-111

Molzen-Corbin & Associates

2701 Miles Road SE
Albuquerque, NM 87106
Phone: (505) 242-5700
Fax: (505) 242-0673
www.molzencorbin.com

Since 1960, Molzen-Corbin has provided innovative engineering and architectural solutions that guide New Mexico's municipalities through growth and change-improving the overall quality of life.

Category: Engineering and Architectural Firm

pp. 178-179

Presbyterian Healthcare Services

2501 Buena Vista SE
Albuquerque, NM 87106
Phone: (505) 923-5700
www.phs.org
info@phs.org

Established in Albuquerque in 1908 as a tuberculosis clinic, Presbyterian is now the largest healthcare services provider in the state of New Mexico, with seven hospitals, fifteen family clinics, and a 280,000-member health plan.

Category: Healthcare Service

pp. 129-131

Private Balloon Flights

9925 Loretta Drive, NW
Albuquerque, NM 87114
Phone: (888) 246-6359 or
(505) 550-2677
www.privateballoonflights.com

Private Balloon Flights is the largest balloon ride operator in the state, offering standard, sweetheart, and group packages complete with ride, brunch, and souvenirs.

Category: Outdoor Activities

p. 167

Public Service Company of New Mexico (PNM)

Alvarado Square
Albuquerque, NM 87158
Phone: (505) 241-4578
Fax: (505) 241-2340
www.pnm.com/econodev

PNM is personally committed to being the most reliable and affordable provider of electricity and gas services for customers throughout New Mexico.

Category: Electricity and Gas Provider

p.83

Ray's Flooring Specialists, Inc.

2241 Phoenix NE
Albuquerque, NM 87107
Phone: (505) 883-1967
Fax: (505) 883-3256
www.raysflooring.com

For over thirty years, strong family values and meticulous attention to customer care has made Ray's Flooring Specialists the top choice of commercial, retail, and builder clients to floor New Mexico.

Category: Flooring Services

pp. 182 - 183

REDW Business and Financial Resources LLC

6401 Jefferson Street, NE
Albuquerque, NM 87199
Phone: (505) 998-3200
Fax: (505) 998-3333
www.redw.com
redw@redw.com

REDW Business and Financial Services LLC is full-service accounting and consulting firm offering expertise in the areas of accounting, tax, auditing, benefits, asset management, financial planning, technology, career placement, and trust.

Category: Accounting and Consulting Firm

pp. 126-127

Rose's Southwest Papers

1701 Second Street Southwest
Albuquerque, NM 87102
Phone: (505) 842-0134
Fax: (505) 242-0342
www.rosessouthwest.com

Since 1984 this family owned and operated business has provided quality paper products to businesses and industries located throughout the United States.

Category: Paper Manufacturer

pp. 220-222

St. Pius X High School

5301 St. Joseph's Drive NW
Albuquerque, NM 87120
Phone: (505) 831-8400
Fax: (505) 831-8413
www.saintpiusx.com

St. Pius X High School combines a dedication to Catholic values with a challenging curriculum to produce future leaders for New Mexico, the nation, and the world.

Category: Education
p. 64

Sutin, Thayer & Browne

Two Park Square, Suite 1000
6565 Americas Parkway NE
Albuquerque, NM 87110
Phone: (505) 883-2500
Fax: (505) 888-6565
www.sutinfirm.com

Since 1946, Sutin, Thayer & Brown has provided Albuquerque and Santa Fe with innovative, aggressive legal services in a wide variety of personal, business, government, real estate, and Internet law.

Category: Legal Services

pp. 122-123

Talbot Financial Corporation

7770 Jefferson NE
Albuquerque, NM 87199
Phone: (505) 828-4000
or (800) 800-5661
Fax (505) 828-0732
www.talbotagency.com
info@talbotagency.com

With sixty offices in twenty states and over $2 billion in annual premiums, Talbot Financial Services consistently ranks among this country's top twenty insurance brokers. Helping clients preserve their property, protect their income and build financial security.

Category: Financial Services

p.96

Technology Ventures Corporation

1155 University Blvd., One Technology Center
Albuquerque, NM 87106
Phone: 505-246-2882
Fax: 505-246-2891
www.techventures.org

Category: High-Tech Business Support

p. 224

TriCore Reference Laboratories

1001 Woodward Place NE
Albuquerque, NM 87102
Phone: 505-938-8888
Fax: 505-938-8977
Toll Free: 800-245-3296
www.tricore.org

Serving New Mexico and the Southwest, TriCore Reference Laboratories is a full-service medical reference laboratory that works with physicians, hospitals and nursing homes, as well as industry for workplace drug testing.

Category: Medical Laboratory

PP. 18-21

United Blood Services of New Mexico

1515 University Boulevard NE
Albuquerque, NM 87102
Phone: (505) 843-6227
(800) 333-8037
Fax: (505) 247-8835
www.unitedbloodservices.org

As a leader in the blood banking industry, United Blood Services of New Mexico provides the people of New Mexico and the Four Corners region with a safe and adequate supply of blood components.

Category: Medical Services

pp. 144-145

The University of New Mexico

1700 Las Lomas NE
Albuquerque, NM 87131
Phone: (505) 277-1989
Fax: (505) 277-8978
www.unm.edu

Nearly 25,000 students annually enroll in the University of New Mexico's more than 200 degree programs at the baccalaureate, graduate, and professional levels.

Category: University

pp.58-62

Victoria's Secret Direct

7001 Zenith Court Northeast
Rio Rancho, NM 87144
Phone: (505)896-6200
Fax: (505) 896-6357
www.victoriassecret.com

This Albuquerque based call center provides Victoria's Secret catalogue customers with optimal service, including bilingual operators twenty-four hours a day, seven days a week.

Category: Retail Service

p. 163

Wells Fargo

200 Lomas Street NW
Albuquerque, NM 87102
Phone: (505) 765-5000
Fax: (505) 765-5191
www.wellsfargo.com

From stagecoaches to the world's leading Internet bank, Wells Fargo has spent 150 years building a great nation by providing financial solutions and community support.

Category: Financial Services

pp. 54-55

Wool Warehouse

First Street and Roma, NW
Albuquerque, NM 87102
Phone: (505) 247-7000
Fax: (505) 247-7025

Once a warehouse bustling with wool textile trade, the Wool Warehouse is now an exciting entertainment venue.

*Category:
Entertainment Venue*

p. 212

Wyndham Albuquerque Hotel

2910 Yale Boulevard, SE
Albuquerque, NM 87106
Phone: (505) 843-7000
Fax: (505) 843-6307
Website: www.wyndham.com

With its award-winning guest service, delicious dining choices, first class rooms, multiple amenities, and meeting space, the Wyndham Albuquerque Hotel offers a uniquely different choice in airport accommodations.

Category: Hotel

pp. 200-201

Editorial Team

Rena Distasio, Senior Writer. Tijeras, New Mexico. A native New Mexican and graduate of the University of New Mexico, freelance writer Rena Distasio contributes articles and reviews on a variety of subjects to regional and national publications. In her spare time she and her husband and three dogs enjoy the great outdoors from their home in the mountains east of Albuquerque.

Charles "Stretch" Ledford, Photographer. Richmond, Virginia. Ledford graduated from the University of North Carolina. As a documentary photographer, Stretch has worked in forty-five countries on five continents. He has received awards from the National Press Photographers' Association, The New York Art Directors' Club, and *Communication Arts* magazine's Photography Annual. In 2001, a series of his photographs were nominated for the Pulitzer Prize. His work can be seen online at www.stretchphotography.com.

John F. Nugent, Photographer. Albuquerque, New Mexico. John F. Nugent has been a professional photographer for more than sixteen years. He studied photography early on at The New York Institute of Photography located in New York City. Assignments have taken him from the streets of midtown Manhattan to colorful South Beach Miami, Florida, and the sun drenched beaches of St. Maarten. His work has appeared in *International Photographer Magazine*, *New York Running News Magazine*, *The Spring Creek Sun Newspaper*, *The Coca-Cola Bottler Magazine*, *Institutional Investor Magazine* and *Dane World Magazine*. His photography is featured in the book *The New York City Marathon—Twenty-Five Years* by Rizzoli Press and an advertising assignment from the Coca-Cola Company has given his work national exposure.

Rod Reilly, Photographer. Atlanta Georgia. Since 1979 Rod has used his training at Carnegie Mellon School of Design, and Rochester Institute of Technology, to create compelling environmental portraits on location of people as they live and work. His clients include Home Depot, Coca Cola USA, United Parcel Service, Cox Communications and McGraw Hill. Starting his career as a staff shooter for Georgia Pacific, Rod has owned his own studio, Reilly Arts & Letters, for the last eleven years, and travels often on assignment. He is a member of A.S.M.P. and the father of three.

Regina Roths, Senior Writer. Andover, Kansas. Roths has written extensively about business since launching her journalism career in the early 1990s. She is a graduate of Wichita State University. Her prose can be found in corporate coffee table books nationally, as well as area magazines, newspapers, and publications. Her love of history and extensive research on various subject matters give her a keen sense of vision for writing.

Alan Weiner, Photographer. Portland, Oregon. Weiner travels extensively both in the United States and abroad, and is a contract photographer for *The New York Times*. He is represented by Gamma/Liaison, and has worked throughout the country on books.

Tim Wright, Photographer. Richmond, Virginia. In his twenty years as a photographer, Wright's assignments have taken him from the Arctic to South Africa and across America. His publishing credits include *Business Week*, *US News & World Report*, *Smithsonian*, *Time*, *Air & Space*, and *The New York Times*. He has a knack for telling a story with each photo.

Chuck Young, Photo Editor and Photographer. Atlanta, Georgia. Young has a degree in photography from the Rochester Institute of Technology in New York, and has more than twenty years experience in photographing such clients as Coca-Cola, NationsBank, BellSouth, and IBM.